NEWMAN, PASCAL, LOISY

AND THE

CATHOLIC CHURCH

Newman, Pascal, Loisy
and
the Catholic Church

BY

W. J. WILLIAMS

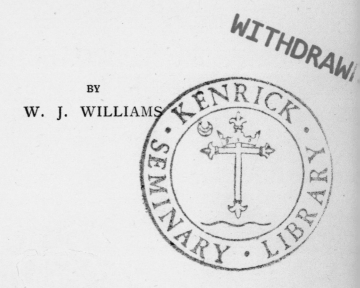

LONDON
FRANCIS GRIFFITHS
34 MAIDEN LANE, STRAND, W.C.
1906

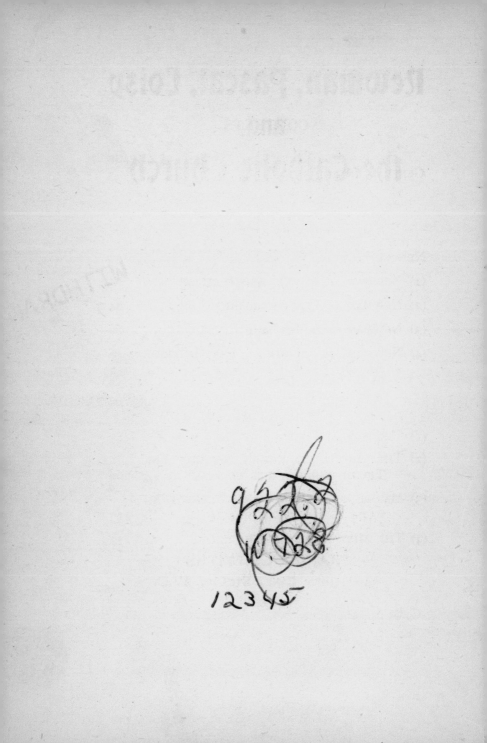

CONTENTS

GENERAL INTRODUCTION.

It is not a little surprising to those who are familiar with the political and religious controversies of some fifty years ago, to observe how seldom what used to be so peremptorily set forth as the right of private judgment is defended, or even mentioned. Indeed, whatever may be our own belief on the subject, this at least must be conceded: that, in some cases without a battle, though after a strenuous and feverish contest in others, the word and the thing have slowly but gradually been pushed out of almost every sphere of thought. Nay more: those entirely personal opinions, those private and particular judgments, —for which the " right " to hold them and insist on them used to be so loudly claimed,—have a tendency to vanish from public discussion, more or less rapidly, in proportion as the persons addressed are more or less educated; and a suspense of judgment which does not venture on an opinion never appears to cease, until it can pass into that scientific certitude which can no longer be counted as opinion at all.

But it is not supposed that the peculiar energy of the intelligence implied in the phrase " to hold an opinion " is now never exercised, or that there is now no room in thought for conclusions which

are only partially formed.   No! but as in many
other matters, so notably in this, the precision of
scientific expression has substituted a clear,
limited idea for a loose and indeterminate one, and
private opinion can now only be expressed in the
modest and intelligible form of an hypothesis.
" Nothing can be done," said M. Pasteur, " without preconceived ideas, only there must be the
wisdom not to accept their deductions beyond what
experience confirms.   Preconceived ideas, subject
to the severe control of experimentation, are the
vivifying flame of scientific observation, while fixed
ideas are its danger."   What is this but to
proclaim that among all thinking men, scientific
hypothesis should be substituted for vague
opinion ?   For the element of vagueness and the
element of fixity which make it impossible to
submit opinions to the test of experiment are
precisely the elements in which the difference
between hypothesis and opinion consists.   Sub-
tract, then, from opinion the element of vagueness
and the element of fixity, and opinion must shrink
into its true proportions, as hypothesis; as such it
must henceforth submit to the rules which scientific
thought demands for all hypotheses alike—be they
good, bad or indifferent, and must be given up
without a murmur so soon as one undoubted fact
is logically adduced against it.

It is not difficult to understand, then, how it
happens that a right of private judgment has come
to be recognized as little better than a right of
personal taste or private fancy; and that scientists

and theologians alike have succeeded in convincing so many, that mere personal opinion is little better than a consequence—fortuitous from one point of view, and inevitable from another—of the environment, physical or mental, hereditary or social, of what are called " units in humanity."

Nor has it been only in science and theology that a tendency of this kind has been observable, but even in matters of art the proverb " every man to his taste " has been felt to be as superficial and anarchical as would be a similar rule in morality or religion. Realism in art and Positivism in history have (no doubt in an exaggerated manner) been insisting ever more and more on the removal of romantic preconception, and purely subjective sentiment or emotion, from pictures and novels and history alike, so that we may know as little as possible of the author's opinions and as much as possible of the facts he intends to portray.

And, though all this has been pressed to such an extent as to become ridiculous and in reality to defeat itself, yet the tendency is but an illustration of the great axiom in all spiritual and intellectual life that " man must die to live "—that individuality must perish in order that personality may survive. " By such self-abnegation," it is urged, " nothing would, in fact, be lost, for the personality of the author or the artist will express itself, if it be a great one, sufficiently for the purposes of art, or the attainment of truth, when his whole energy is employed in conveying to mankind whatever is true and important in accordance with the ascertained laws—which are necessary to lucid expression—the laws of order, symmetry and balance.''

But if such criticism is felt barren and pernicious in matters of art, far more obvious is the danger in morality, and as the state insists upon certain laws necessary to the well-being of society, so men have begun to feel that there must be, however difficult it may be to attain them, ascertainable and universal laws for the higher degrees of morality and what has been called '' perfection.''   The vague rhetoric of Sallust, the austere moral of Tacitus, as well as the brilliant special pleading of Macaulay, are felt to be unscientific, and, in some sense, arbitrary and personal, as giving a false value to important elements in life short of that law—truly universal— which should become clear from a mere adherence to facts.   If morality, for instance, is, indeed, the important element in life we think it, a strict relation of the facts will sufficiently prove it to be so ; but, on the other hand, if it is not, an impartial account of things as they are is the only means we have of discovering what in fact the due place of morality is.   And it will scarcely be denied that the arrangement of facts in such a form as '' to point a moral '' has begun by bringing discredit upon history and ended by bringing doubt upon what the historian considered to be morality.

The first tendency, therefore, of scientific historians has been to ignore '' all moral landmarks "—as Lord Acton observes was done in the latest history of the French Revolution.   And it is not too much to say that we have already left behind a history such as that of Carlyle, while the immense empire of scientific criticism is slowly beginning to enclose the whole domain of history as but one of its more important departments.

If we cannot bring ourselves to see things as they are—it is urged—so much the worse for us. Nothing for us should be good or bad, beautiful or hideous—on any *a priori* basis of old fashioned metaphysic or in accordance with some physical accident of heredity.   We should but take things as we find them; unlearn our arbitrary likings and disgusts, and attempt no more to measure them by an absolute ideal—the result and the cause alike of misconception and personal bias.   In other words, scientific thought insists that we should allow no further weight to our private judgment than may justly be assigned, by the logic of facts, to a unit in humanity.

But it is clear that if such reasoning as this may be applied to history and to art it must be applied to thought likewise, and, therefore, to conduct.   And to a certain extent this has been attempted and has been accomplished.   Men have taken the law of the state as simply a physical fact, obeyed it, and cut off completely all the more delicate and interesting parts of morality as belonging to what possibly might turn out to be the mere dreams of former ages.   They have taken from life all variety and richness, and reduced it to

its barest possible expression in order to begin
again or start fair, as they would express it.   And,
in a certain sense, they had a logical right to do
so.   The only question was this: whether they
did not merely lose the habits which would come
by acting in accordance with the more delicate and
interesting conceptions of morality which   came
from former ages, while they gained nothing but
a void?   It was quite clear, indeed, that private
judgment and personal bias had been extended too
far, and ought to be limited; but the   question
remained—limited by what?   And if yielded up to
whom should they be yielded?   It was plain that
there must be, at least, a   provisional   morality
beyond the mere orderings of the state; but what
was there in the world to provide it?

But if the demand for an objective criticism
has been made in such subjects as   history,
literature and art, much more is it required where
science, which has been the cause of the whole
movement, has been practically concerned.   In
the middle ages science was considered and was
called the hand-maiden of Theology, Theology the
Queen of the sciences: and science came to be
treated often as if it existed but to illustrate and
enforce religious truths.

No one can say that it is thus treated now.   It
is perceived, at last, that the progress of science
requires for its rapidity and completeness total
independence of assumption and dictation from
without and especially the assumptions or dictation
of theology.   And this conviction has arisen not

because theology is considered false or doubtful (though that consideration has of course influenced many) but because the inter-weaving of two lines of thought so diverse is a process which gives too many opportunities for the play of prejudice and personal opinion, fixed interpretations of texts, and mis-representations of facts, for the security either of science or religion. But even now scientific men are continually causing a shock to those religious minds which hear of their conclusions without having followed their process. The scientific man has long ago perceived, and, therefore, in season and out of season insists, that it is his duty, in the department of research that he has selected, to account for things as they are, only by means of facts to which he can relate them. He cannot allow to supersede his investigations any account of them which appeals, for its ¹'dity, to some principle which he is unable sc¹ to recognise. When he cannot accoun. or an event (whether it be the origin of t. ..u or the appearance of miracle) to give up the attempt to account for it would, he considers, be nothing else but to forsake his post. Why should he, as a scientific man, suddenly set aside the inductive method which, by its very nature, renews its strength and increases its bulk every day, for some final axiom or dogma which would shut up the subject for ever? Why should he be compelled to express his belief in a proposition while it is still possible for him, on scientific grounds, to suspend his judgment and thereby to leave open the path to future discovery? To do anything else, he argues, would be to outrun the facts with which it is his business, as a man of science, accurately and steadily to keep pace. He must not pretend that he has found a solution until he can demonstrate it, and he is bound always to be searching for a solution in terms of the science to which the problem intrinsically belongs. He has no right, he contends, to close a question in science, or to assert to the scientists of the future that *his* investigation is final or that he has arrived at the miraculous.

When a learned scientist, then, is quoted by Lord Salisbury (to take a well-known instance) as acquiescing for the time in a theory which he admits to be inadequate, on the ground that, should he not do so, he would be compelled to have recourse to the theological or miraculous account of creation, he was but saying what, after all, a scientific man as such is bound to say—what, in another context the Schoolmen, centuries ago, regarded as axiomatic—what, indeed, before the Schoolmen, St. Augustine had implied in his letter to Faustus, that we are bound to remain within the limits of the natural until we are ejected, as it were, by force; that we should examine every cause conceivable before we admit a final cause and acknowledge every secondary cause until we are thrown, of necessity, upon a first. But never, by science, can we be compelled to admit a first or final cause; for such a cause is beyond the ken of science, as it is beyond the scope of induction.

You cannot get the infinite from any number of finites, nor can man by searching find out God.

"But how is it," one may naturally enquire, "that a principle admitted in the days of St. Thomas and St. Augustine has only become the practice now, and that even in our own days the practice should to some extent become a scandal?" It is because the consequences of the principle were not fully understood nor generally expected until they actually arrived. It has been with induction and the scientific method (which is something far more complete than induction) as with all great principles and modes of thought, whether they concern political liberty or social advancement or scientific progress. It has needed opposition to give it precision and circumstances to show its importance, and time to exhibit the width of its sphere. It has been the accumulation of facts and the progress of events which have added, as it were while men slept, to the volume of its evidence and the scope of its energy. It has slowly undermined authoritative statement and ancient tradition by no purposed onset, by no premeditated attack, but by the inevitable progress of discovery—perhaps in departments of thought apparently diverse altogether from those in which its distinctive qualities are ultimately most remarked. The scientific method in great part existed and was worked long before Christendom was formed; and then lay embedded in the philosophy of Aristotle side by side with propositions which the least learned and the least capable of scientists can now refute by the simplest of its applications.   It is now not only a method which can be used, it has created an atmosphere which can be felt; and facts almost seem to suggest their own classification as discovery slowly increases their number, and carefully sets forth their qualities.   No longer marshalled under arbitrary titles given them by some philosopher who finds them natural or unnatural, præternatural or supernatural, according to the length of his experience or the amount of his learning,—or, on a basis no more secure, divides them into genera and species—they have forced upon the modern mind the suspicion that generalization can be but provisional and classification temporary.

Now the principle of induction not only existed long ago in the philosophy of Aristotle, but has been constantly inculcated and implicitly followed by the Christian religion wherever it has been in contact with actual conduct (its main and true concern) and the spiritual life.   The minding of small things, the condescension to detail; "the falling in love," as St. Paul literally expresses it "with little " facts, the taking things one by one; the very practice of humility : these are, after all, but the method of induction carried into ethics*. That the laborious and indefatigable study of detail will be more successful in the attainment of the truth than the confident assertion and abstract discussion of principles is an axiom that answers so clearly to the teaching of Christianity upon conduct that it needs but the comparison to make us feel that it is the same law in a different guise. In each case the evil to be got rid of is the "*Ego*," which with its preconceptions and self-sufficiency does what is right in its own eyes, judges itself by its own laws and makes itself the centre of the universe.

So again, Lord Bacon in speaking of the freedom necessary for science from all the old idolatries, is consciously using language analogous to that of the old spiritual books, when he bids us, in effect, become fools that we may be wise; become little that we may be great; and put away the self-made idols of our pride, the idol of the market-place, the idol of the theatre, the idol of the tribe.

But modern philosophy does not allow us to stop here, or, on the part of science, to plead for the complete overthrow of preconception and philosophical hypothesis—preconception which is the very life of scientific enquiry " without which," says Pasteur, " nothing can be done." And, indeed, no fact is more widely admitted by philosophers of every school as well as by men of science than that induction alone has never led to any discovery at all. It is, surely significant that the notion of private judgment should find its profoundest condemnation here and that those writers (whether Bacon or his shallower admirers) who have wished to give the freest scope to honest enquiry should find themselves compelled to give to self, to the "*ego*," to the private judgment, an ever smaller scope till it has reached the point at

B

which Catholic theologians consider it to be
necessary in the acceptance of any authority
whatever; and the Apostolic saying that no
Scripture is of private interpretation is felt to be
true not only of sacred books but of all history,
literature, and science; of all facts, indeed, with
which it is possible for the mind of man to become
acquainted.

And consequently modern thought has very
generally come to recognize the necessity for the
attitude of the church of the Middle Ages towards
science. "The sense of the whole," as we hear
repeated so often, "must come first"; and with
philosophy as a whole, with the moral and religious
basis of life the church of the Middle Ages was
obliged to concern itself. It is not necessary to
say that such an attitude was justifiable: the
limitations of the energy of man rendered some
such attitude inevitable. It was inevitable (and
Positivists now generally not only admit but
contend that it was so) that, in an age in which
men felt the first, the deepest, and the immediate
necessity to be some uniform ethical and religious
ideal, science should remain in the background.
Who can tell how perilous to civilization, as a
whole, might not have been the possession of
scientific knowledge, independent of any fixed
religion or code of morals, by a half barbarous
community of all kinds of races: with a social life
scarcely begun, with the anti-social forces scarcely
subdued, with a general character as wild, fierce
and ungovernable as that of a modern anarchist?

What might not have happened to society, if a kind of knowledge which certainly means power, but, as certainly, need not mean social virtue or self-restraint, had given to large masses of men the self-sufficiency and independence which belong, and to some extent rightly belong, to scientific authority now? There can be little doubt, indeed, that science might, for a time, have progressed with greater rapidity; but civilization, on its humane and social side, could hardly have been reached at all; nor, as time went on, could science itself have progressed in security without the aid and protection of that general culture which could not have been obtained apart from the influence, and even the conservative bias, of religion.

Few, probably, will deny that the Catholic Church in the Middle Ages was the sole, as she was the inevitable, representative of human solidarity in Europe. But it is to some such living representative of human solidarity that all these tendencies away from merely individual judgments, tastes, and fancies to which we have alluded, are already pointing. To the acknowledged conclusions of mankind as a whole, so far as these conclusions can be represented, is the allegiance of man felt to be logically due; with these he must start; to these he must, even though it be long after his work on earth has been accomplished, ultimately yield. He himself does but come as a single tone in a vast harmony of which he forms a part; and the matured judgment of mankind is the sole criterion left him not only for the validity of the methods

which he uses, but of his sanity in the conduct of
life; not only of the conclusions which he draws or
the premises from which he argues, or the
language (certainly not invented by himself) in
which he thinks, but even of his physical construc-
tion in brain and body; for by that alone can he be
judged to be human at all.   It was because this
human solidarity can alone give authority to final
judgments or become an ultimate court of appeal
that the Church was forced to attempt its realization
on such a scale as was then possible.   She came
forward (little as she realized what she did) not as
the representative of fixed ideas but as the representative of great religious preconceptions and,
all unconsciously submitted them to the severe
control of experimentation in the life of the world
and of action.   She came forward as the representative for man, for the individual, of the vast
ethical and religious process which had slowly been
growing up in the human family for so long.   She
came forward as representing (so far as she could
gather it) the sum of the religious idea in humanity,
for the unit.   She became the organism, so far
as was possible, in which the religious process was
to be carried out.   She gave to man " preconceptions " which, as they are " the life of science "—
so are they the life of religion, of thought, of
conduct and of art.   She gave the rules by which
man destroys his selfish individuality, but creates
the personality which survives.

   That the general movement of thought in
Europe is favourable to some such ultimate

tribunal as the Catholic Church would be, could men be convinced that some such ideal as that which is suggested by the name, is, in the Catholic Church, actually realized, has been acknowledged by some, who feel the danger of living without at least a provisional representative of solidarity, in morals and religion. Such persons have acknowledged that (whatever its defects) the Catholic Church does provide for the individual such a basis for morality and religion; and this, not on some private view of things, but in the name and on the authority of as large a body of men in all nations as she has been able to concentrate upon the task. Her Catholicism is felt to be even more than what she herself has claimed. It has come in the process of time, and by contact with every kind of national tradition—in morals, in religion and even in philosophy—to be a Catholicism not only of Christian tradition but, to some extent, of the whole great religious tradition in the human family. To such persons it has sometimes occurred that the Church may be not only " heir by default " to the great councils of the fourth century, but " heir by default " to all former representatives of the religious principle in whatever nation or century such representatives are to be found. And if, on the one hand, some such authority exists in the world at all, there is, on the other, little doubt that some such authority has become an elementary necessity in an age which hopes or seems to hope, while resolving into its component parts the ground on which the human race is standing, that the time is about to arrive in which it will be possible for every man to stand without difficulty on nothing at all.

Nor is it a long step for those who have come to regard the individual as a unit in humanity to go on to regard humanity itself as a unit in that universe whose limits are unknown. The isolation of the unit in humanity throws him upon the larger unit of which he feels himself a part, and hence the desire for an authority objective, cosmopolitan, catholic; a centre of unity and a common ground for thought. The latitudinarian, the liberalistic, and individualist view of truth as something dependent upon our subjective conception of it has disappeared as completely as the notion that truth can be said to be something lying, as it were, outside the human race, as something "sole and unapproachable."

Thus it was that Newman's opposition to latitudinarianism and his subjective idealism drove him from opposite sides into the line which he ultimately took. Truth cannot be considered as simply dependent upon the individual nor yet can it be set outside the only possible instrument of its expression : revelation was not made simply from outside, but grew up also from within. The truth which makes us free and which causes a religion to prevail is not a something without ourselves alone, but is only to be recognized as something objective because it is immanent in the human race as a whole, and is inherent in all things from the first. And thus, truth being something which is

as it were born with the human race, it may be
said "to live" in it and have its habitation with
the sons of men. If it lives, it grows; and growth
is the test of its life. A particular kind of truth
admits of being represented by a particular kind of
process; and, as the cosmic process may be said in
one sense to give birth to truth, so truth—still
acting within the same laws but on a new plane—
may be said to live and grow in a process ethical
or religious, in such sense that you cannot appeal
to any "truth" outside to condemn it.

If, then, we find that the old bases for the
ethical idea and the religious idea are slowly being
set on one side—not as simply untrue but as impossible to the present conditions of thought
(because a question having once been scientifically
opened cannot be theologically shut)—is it not of
some importance to consider whether we may not
be able to get rid of these question begging bases
for society and religion, and substitute for them a
basis which can be recognised by mankind in the
present state of its consciousness as the philosophy
of the schools was recognised by Europe in a past
state of its consciousness? Can we not express in
terms of the thought of our day what the schoolmen considered it their duty to express in terms of
the thought of theirs? If the scholastic philosophy
represented one aspect of the solidarity of Christendom, and the transition which this age is accom-
plishing is a transition to a newer and a wider, the
time has certainly now arrived in which the transition must be fully realized. For such a transition

can never be completed unless it is consciously undergone and carried out both by the religious and scientific thought of the day : for this purpose there must be a solidarity in time as well as in space; there must be continuity or else there will be no growth.   Now a preliminary necessity for meeting this continuity is clearly some Catholic organisation; but, whatever claim Catholics may make for the Catholic Church, it is certain that in humanity at large this break in continuity has occurred.   It is useless to attempt to bridge over the past by some artificial arrangement. How is it possible to make use of the Catholic Church even if this be the use to which it should be put ?   How is it possible for those who hold that the existence of God, for instance, can never be proved, to belong to a Church whose fundamental article of belief is His existence ? How can those who reject the miraculous as an absurdity believe in the existence of a miraculous Church ? Does not the Church compel us to receive all the question-begging bases for Society which Society has rejected ?

These questions show only too clearly into what a state of confusion the whole religious question has been flung by the ignorance of well-meaning persons, both on the side of religion and against it. The dogmas of the Church even on the existence of God and the nature of miracle have come to be represented as fixed ideas—the bane of science and an obstacle to progress, rather than testimonies to the exigencies of man's nature and fruitful preconceptions essential to his growth.

In this manner such declarations as that of the Vatican Council on the existence of God (where it is laid down that this can be proved by the natural reason alone) have been so interpreted as to make the conversion of modern society to the Church simply impossible. Whereas the article in question was clearly intended to be consistent with the fact that belief in the existence of God in the Church's sense is very difficult outside the Church; that many of the early Christians, before they entered the Church, were in precisely the same condition of mind as modern society, and that to the majority of converts in many ages the idea of God as a Person and as one who rewards and punishes was revealed for the first time by the Christian Church.

If it be asked, then, " How can modern society, which rejects the existence of a Personal God, accept the authority of a Church the first article of whose creed proclaims His existence?" We may ask in turn, " How did ancient society, in a similar condition, accept that authority?" What converts to Christianity were in search of then, was probably what all men who think, are in search of now : not some abstractly perfect proof, not some mathematical or scholastic demonstration, not some truth *behind* phenomena, not some fixed idea; but life—life of a kind so central to the nature of man as to give life to all the spheres of his thought and action. If he has found this life for himself, he has found God and the absolute; the ultimately real—that which really makes to live; he has found the truth—not as an abstraction nor even as an abstract ideal—but as something that lives with his own life and grows with his own energies.

Now it is religion and morality which are concerned with the sources of life. Where, then, is he to look for such life? Is he to find it without or within? He is to find it both within and without, in whatever has life or contributes to life. He must derive his moral and religious life from the moral and religious process as he derived his physical life from the cosmic process.

In looking for that religion which is to contribute to his religious life from without, how is he to choose?

On the grounds on which we have been discussing the subject hitherto, he may reject every religion whose essential characteristic fails of the notion of universal solidarity and organic unity; which is not an organism and which is not, in any sense alive; which performs none of the functions of an organism; because, as humanity becomes conscious of itself as a unit in the universe, all religions that are merely national or are connected with any basis not universal become impossible. No religion whose characteristic mark is not the endeavour to get a universal basis of all religious truth can be admitted into his enquiry, and no religion which sets any insuperable obstacle to the gaining such a basis can be admitted.

A brilliant opponent of the Catholic Church complains that Cardinal Newman deals only with the Christian religion and leaves out altogether the great religions, for instance, of the East; and he conceives Newman's answer to have been that the superior civilization of the West may fairly be considered a sufficient reason for so doing.   But Newman's real answer is far deeper than that. The very basis and mode of development of those religions has always tended to obscure that kind of Catholicity which, in the Christian religion, has enabled it to absorb such elements from other religions as it needs.   But, according to Newman, that first thing that man requires of the religion of which he is in search, is that its basis should be of such a kind as to enable it to assimilate all the moral and spiritual truths that are found in other religions.   Such a basis he considered he had found in a Church whose chief characteristic and essential note is its Catholicity.   Though that Catholicity at first did but mean the Catholicity of its own traditions, Newman found in the Church's capacity for assimilation a proof of the very kind of Catholicity we now require; for it has even been made a reproach to the Catholic Church that she absorbed the traditions of all the nations with which she came in contact, and that she continues to assimilate both truth and method from without.

If there be a great religious tradition in the world, whencesoever it arose, it must have its part in the development of man.   Whether we choose to consider it as having arisen out of the great cosmic process and, therefore, as forming a part of that process still; or whether it be supposed to be in some unknown manner broken off from the cosmic process; anyhow, a religious process there is, nor can any sophistry convince us that what has once made a part and an essential part of the whole man can be taken from him without an essential loss, unless it is, in some manner replaced by what is better.

But if the religious tradition of humanity becomes a mere matter of individual opinion that loss has occurred; for, to man, as such, religion would then have become a mass of confusion, arbitrary theory and personal caprice, in short, not only a mystery but a mystery without any real relation to his life. Religion would, in this case, have sunk into a mere enigma, a hopeless puzzle. And we know that men of equal capacity and of equal piety (so far as we can allow ourselves to be their judge) have come to completely opposite conclusions with regard to its significance; have belonged to opposing sects, parties, and religions; or, even have given up religion altogether in consequence of its divisions. The break in continuity, then, to which we have made reference, has issued in complete anarchy of opinion.

We cannot get at the significance of the religious tradition, for the religious tradition itself, if held at all, is held not only in contention, but in contradiction.

At this point in the argument, however, we are sometimes reassured by being told that " in *essentials* the religious tradition remains significant for man." He can, it is supposed, pierce through and eliminate the differences and arrive at the bed-rock beneath by the use of his intellectual powers or his spiritual discernment. Now this might be simply denied (as it often has been), for it is clear that those who have thus used their intellect have differed as to what the *essential part of religion* is as often as religions differ from one another : some bringing " what is essential " down to conceptions so vague that others can find in them no meaning at all.

If again, somebody asserts that his particular view is the true one, and that what he conceives to be essential to religion is alone essential, whether he is a philosopher or a sectary, he lays himself open to the absurdity of attempting to found religious truth on personal opinion ; and all other philosophers and sectaries may speak of their own views with the same confidence and in the same manner. And yet even to this day persons who consider themselves philosophers, without even the excuse of the fanatic, who conceives himself personally guided by God, will often set to work to divide the " precious from the base " in religion ; as if some standard of what is precious in religion set up in a few years by themselves were of equal validity with the natural process of evolution and survival of the fittest. This is about as wise as to affirm that we can know by instinct or by inspiration something which is hidden from the rest of mankind ; nor have philosophers been a whit wider minded or less arbitrary

and provincial than the most insular of English
Protestants in condemning what they do not
happen to like or judging by the kind of instinct
that is simply the product of their environment.
Every man in these matters does and will always
answer according to his personal opinions, his
race-feelings, his temperament, the philosophic
system he knows best, his particular hopes, aspirations, and knowledge. Up to a certain point he is
bound to do so, and ought to do so. Here, however, if anything in the world is clear, it is clear
that he needs an answer which will be universal in
its significance, because he himself cannot now
believe in a religion which is really his own invention and can, in no sense, stand above him, a
religion judged by personal instinct and opinion
alone, a religion of individual eclecticism.

No certain answer, then, will be given to this
question at all, except in the points where purely
scientific knowledge will slowly force consent on
the whole of mankind, and upon Catholics as well
as others. Where the answer from philosophy is
merely hypothetical, it may justly be advanced;
but, in the meantime, the religious tradition must
persist or perish, and mere hypothesis is not
sufficient to kill it; nor, on the other hand (apart
from the confirmation of ages of conscious practical working) sufficient to keep it alive.

In those cases of dogma in which philosophy
cannot advance further than opinion, or, indeed,
as generally happens, mere arbitrary like or dislike, an answer such as we require is impossible.

In those cases of dogma in which scientific facts have made the philosophic answer scientifically certain the answer is of profound moment to the Church and must, at last, be absorbed by her. But, in the meantime, for the individual who seeks a religion such an answer, in a particular case, may be interesting and enlightening, but it will not give him the religion he seeks; it will not bring him at once to the deeper sources of the religious life of humanity; it will not put him into direct contact with the religious process in man.

But, after all, the answer to the question: " What is essential to religion ?" is, surely, itself essential. And yet it is clear that individuals differ as much on this point as on any other, as much as they differ on questions such as that of justification, or the Divinity of Christ, or the existence of God, or the necessity for religion at all. Nevertheless, so long as this question is not answered it is plain that a religion of what people call " essentials " is no religion.

As necessary, then, as religion is to man, so necessary to religion is such an organism as will gather together into one, express and report progress upon, the development of whatever is inevitably religious in man's nature.

Now to that solution of the problem which would find in some actual Church such an organism and such a mode of expression and development as we have shown to be desirable, there are made many preliminary objections which we shall now endeavour to meet.

It is said, then, that when such a Church demands the submission of mankind to her definitions of what is essential, she does but make one essential doctrine instead of many to which it is, at least, as difficult to assent as to the others. It is as difficult to believe in the authority of the Church as to believe in any of the doctrines laid down as essential by the sects. It is as difficult to believe in the Church as in Baptismal Regeneration. It does but put the difficulty further back to ask us to believe by one act of the will, instead of asking us to believe, by many acts, one by one.

Such an objection is intended to cut away the root idea of authority in religion; but even those philosophers who trust most to the individual reason are obliged to trust first in the general; and those who have gone furthest into the region of pure thought have been compelled to begin with a language and a brain; while those sectaries who imagine that they believe in certain Christian mysteries, on the direct authority of God, will acknowledge that those mysteries have never been, and, from their very nature, never could be, proved, as mysteries, to their private judgment, one by one. They accept them, as they think, on the authority of God.

Religious mysteries and religious truths may be ideas on their way to realization; half revealed and half concealed in the instinctive language of symbol and metaphor. Such truths, I say, may be on their way to a clearer expression and may some day admit of proof; but as they stand, they are

dim, difficult, and remote. It has been owing to
this fact that Christianity has been regarded
always by the majority of Christians as a " revelation." It was regarded as a " revelation " because,
while it made an appeal on external grounds to
human reason, it internally transcended human
reason. And so, in some sense, religion always
must be regarded; because its origin, from a
simply natural point of view, is exceedingly
difficult to trace. Those who find its origin in
fetish worship forget that things must be judged
by what they become; they do not make religion
as it is any less important, but show that fetish
worship was more important than we are asked to
suppose it.

Externally, however, the authority of the
Church rests upon a fact in nature. As such it
may be regarded, nor is it necessary to the proof of
the basis on which the Church stands to prove it to
have any supernatural character at all. If *a*
religion is essential to man's full development; if,
when he comes to realise that there are different
religions, he perceives that one must be better than
the others; if, in order to find out the best, he
essentially needs some exterior sign or notes of its
qualities and some interior criterion of what is
essential *to itself*; then an objective religion, " a
proponent " of religious doctrine, here and now
and ever present, is essential to religion. Again,
if a religious tradition exists in humanity, and
separated religions such as those of the nations
before Christianity, have become conscious that

they cannot each be simply the universal religion; then an authority to define what is essential to such a religion as *shall* be universal, is essential to religion itself and to the carrying on of the religious process in the world. The authority, then, of such a church as really carries out this ideal, would rest on the same foundation as religion itself; and the necessity of religion itself to man can only be established by arguments which are, at the same time, establishing hers.

So that to say that the doctrine of the authority of the Church is as difficult to believe in as the particular religious doctrines proposed to our belief is to mistake the nature of the problem. The authority of the Church, as it first comes to us, is a perfectly natural phenomenon, founded on reasons which appeal to us on perfectly natural grounds, so long as we believe that we have no right to make a break in the continuity of a developing idea and tradition on which man has hitherto set a high value; whereas the religious doctrines, which are proposed to our belief by a religion professing to be revealed, come to us, as each of them beyond the power of our reason to prove, as is clear from the fact that they are supposed to demand faith.

And here it is necessary to observe what I have already shown must be granted, that the Church so conceived does not put an end to the use of the speculative intelligence: it does but lay down those laws for its exercise which are necessary to the very existence of the religious idea. It does not forbid analysis, explanation or the philosophic account of the history of religion, or the mode of acceptance of its dogmas inevitable in philosophic enquiry. It does not remove the right of scientific doubt. It does but involve the demand that this religious tradition shall be dealt with as a fact, which must be acknowledged as existing in humanity as truly as the passion of love exists in humanity and with the same sort of right to be there; and that consequently to attempt its removal without substitute is as absurd as to attempt the removal of the passion of love.

But if such an authority as that which has been described be essential to the survival and development of religion, the question remains: Where is that authority to be found? It is clear that a tribunal which is to exercise such authority must have the means of exercising it, must have some organ of expression: must have a voice. If the voice or power of expressing or modifying religious ideas or traditions were in abeyance, the very function of such a tribunal could no longer be exercised.

Now the only substitute for a living tribunal of the kind, which is proposed in modern Europe, by High Church Anglicans in one sense and by German critics in another, is what is called the Primitive Church. It is considered that the Christian Church in the days of its early purity (variously defined as a period of from twenty years to six centuries) is sufficiently clear in its teaching and, at the same time, sufficiently deep and broad to be appealed to as an arbiter in all disputes, while it has, at the same time, those characteristics of Catholic religion essential to the requirements of the modern mind. But apart from the fact that it is not Catholic in time, and therefore cannot absorb new ideas, the Primitive Church, taken as an authority in the present has not sufficient objective clearness for such a purpose; for it is admitted, on all hands, that it is impossible that any modern Church should be simply a fascimile of the Primitive. A man brought up with Roman Catholic proclivities will say that the Primitive Church, though not exactly like the modern Catholic Church, yet was implicitly and virtually what that Church is now. Had the Fathers lived to see how simply necessary to the Church is infallibility in its Head they would, such persons contend, have been ready explicitly to declare what even in their own day they seem sometimes to imply or, at least, to anticipate. Another, brought up in Anglican surroundings, will say that though the Primitive Church cannot be called simply Anglican, yet it was implicitly and virtually far more like the Anglican Church than any other; and, if the Fathers had lived to see the disastrous effects of Papal usurpation, there cannot be any doubt what Church in Europe they would consider in doctrine nearest their own. And, moreover, if one is ready to set back the Primitiveness and purity of the Christian Church a little further— Calvinists, Methodists, Congregationalists, Quakers and all the rest are ready to make the

same claim for their respective communions. One
will hold that the form of government, in the early
Church, was implicitly an aristocracy, another
that it was democratic; others that it was
(implicitly) monarchical, and some that it was
(implicitly) all three.

And even, when writers belonging to any
Christian communion become scientific historians,
they are inclined to believe that it is of the very
genius and essence of the Church that what it was
once in form, *that* it must ever remain, or that any
difference found to exist between it and a modern
form of Christianity ought to be considered fatal to
the modern *form*, unless it is in a matter " non-
essential !" Having come to this conclusion, they
go on to show that it is impossible to say *what* is
non-essential, if the point happens to be one in
which they are interested. If, however, the point
is one which does *not* interest them, then they pronounce it non-essential at once, as if *ex cathedra*
and on the concurrent authority of a thousand
streams of tradition. We must endeavour, at
least, to find an authority which does not labour
under the preliminary difficulty of not being an
authority at all, or of being an authority only *in
posse* and by implication and with the " *due* use "
of " the private judgment," and then only in what
we choose to consider " essentials."

What is called the Branch Theory labours
under the similar difficulty that it is impossible, at
the very outset, to gain the required authority for
believing that any one branch of the Church is

what it pretends to be.   It is nothing but the
Catholic Church, taken as a whole, which can pronounce which are its parts and which are not parts
of it, and those who hold the theory are among the
strongest exponents and upholders of the fact.
The Branch Theory requires a living authority to
pronounce whether it is in agreement with the
whole tradition of the Church with regard to what
is essential to the *form* of the Church as much as
any other Theory or doctrine.

Thus, if there be anything essential in religion
at all (essential, I mean, to man's full development) we must, at least, know what religion is.
And if we cannot define it; if it seems to be something which is still in the process of realising
itself, it is essential for us that we should put ourselves in communication with its living representative and the real sources of its life.

Some such Church as the Catholic Church
claims to be is, then, " heir by default " to that
authority   which   belonged   once   to   national
religions (so far forth as a merely national religion
can ever be an authority), but can now no longer
belong   to   religions   merely   national,   however
valuable   the   separated   truths   found   in   various
nations.

When the ideal or religious element in man
had once come to be expressed in men, it became
a process, and this, again, became slowly but more
and   more   definitely   an   organism   in   which   the
process was carried on.   Man summed up in it,
and   expressed   by   it   what   he   had   found,   by

experience, to be his inevitable attitude towards religion, towards the infinite, towards all that he calls God and worships. He summed up in it, and he expressed by it a particular sort of truth—truth of experience—in which he related his religious conceptions to the different stages of his growth in thought. Add, then, to the notion of a particular kind of *truth*, its development and life in a particular kind of organism (becoming ever more clearly one and conscious of itself), and you will see that if once we have gained the only possible organism, that organism by selecting what is food for it, and rejecting what is poison (as other organisms do) is, in this case, selecting what is *religiously true* and rejecting what is *religiously false*. Not only, therefore, does the religious individual find it necessary to recognise a sort of provisional and relative infallibility in his moral sense (as it is called) if he is to have any character at all, but a religious organism must have had, if it has continued to live, this relative infallibility in selecting what was food for it and rejecting what was poison.

But as it is a conscious organism, an organism consciously one, it must know, and imply by its acts the knowledge that it has this power, inasmuch as it knows that it lives and continues to grow. The claim to this relative infallibility, therefore, becomes one of the essential notes or marks of the religious organism of which we are in search. In other words, as we saw before, it is the first essential of religious authority that it should

be able to answer with religious infallibility the
question : What is essential to religion ?

Though we cannot trust the religious element
in man outside its sphere, any more than we
should trust our physical senses outside their
sphere, yet there is as much reason to trust the
religious element within a sphere which it has built
up and made for itself, as to trust the physical
senses in a sphere which is clearly their own.
" Let us make for the truth," then, " with the
whole man," and not arbitrarily leave out of sight
so positive an element in his history as his
religion. Let us make ourselves one with the only
representative of the religious process in the world
which has at once a potential universality and a
claim to continuity with the past.   Such is the
external or traditionalistic argument for the
Catholic religion which lies implicitly indeed, in the
works of Cardinal Newman—but whose nature has
been misunderstood because it is supposed to
exclude, as well as to prescind from, all rational
metaphysic and to substitute authority for the use
of the reason. How far it does so and in what
sense it is modified by Newman himself we shall
see hereafter.

NEWMAN, PASCAL, LOISY
AND THE CATHOLIC CHURCH.

PART I

NEWMAN.

It was the fortune of Cardinal Newman all through his life that he was compelled by the position which he occupied, to address himself, for the most part, to men without any philosophic training, or with a very narrow one, on subjects which require a philosophic terminology and systematic treatment. He was attempting to do the work at the same time of a statesman and a philosopher, a man of action and a theologian. He desired to waken once more to life, in the Church of England, the vigorous theology of Bull, of Hooker, of Jeremy Taylor, of Laud, and to induce Churchmen to throw themselves back upon what he regarded as the only position which could be logically and consistently defended. But he desired to do more. He desired to set forth the whole of that theology in a manner at once so luminous and so lucid that there would be henceforth little chance of its falling into that neglect and confusion in which he found it. And for this purpose it was necessary to go back to the sources from which it professed to have been derived, to the great Fathers of the earlier centuries and to the history of the early Church. In addition, therefore, to his regular labours on essays and sermons, he translated St. Athanasius as well as writing the " Prophetical Office of the Church," while he joined, with indomitable energy, in the effort that was then being made, to bring the Church of the Fathers clearly before English readers. The amount of energy and labour expended in this part of the work which he had set himself would have been enough to fill the life of many an able and energetic writer.

But this was by no means all that he attempted or all that he accomplished. He wrote on philosophical subjects also, and attempted to build for his theory a philosophical, as well as a theological, foundation. It is with these philosophical opinions that I shall be, for the most part, concerned in the pages I am about to write.

Such a task as that which Newman had attempted, under the conditions which modern life imposes, was, from the first, sufficiently difficult: but when it is realized how narrow and unsatisfactory was the philosophic training at Oxford in those days, and how strangely antiquated was the philosophical training of the majority of those with whom, in his later years, he was compelled to contend, it is not to be wondered at if philosophers are apt to regard him as little better than an ecclesiastical advocate with a dash of poetic mysticism, and ecclesiastics (both Catholic and Protestant) as a dangerous sceptic and an over subtle philosopher.

On the other hand, the time seems at last to have arrived when the unfairness of reaction in that later Oxford school in which " the star of Newman " was said to have set " the sun of Mill to have arisen " has itself slowly died away or is, at any rate, in the process of dying. Men have gradually come to acknowledge that the narrowness of training and a certain almost Puritanic gloom from which Newman suffered throughout his life, yet did not prevent him from reaching nearer than others that bed rock on which alone stand all the " tower'd cities " of man's passionate aspiration, and, among them, the city of God. We might, indeed, well afford to forget the unfairness had it not, here and there, been given a plausibility and a chance of permanence by the inevitable looseness and apparent inconsistency of writings so various and so frequently " occasional " as those of Newman. It must then, be our endeavour to find what is the origin of the unfairness with which he has sometimes been treated: what is the nature of the misrepresentation to which he has been subjected; in what the permanent value of his philosophical opinions consists.

It would be impossible for any man living to go through all that has been written, or answer all the objections that have been raised, against works dealing with subjects so difficult, so complex and so numerous. While the unfairness and bias of reaction lasted (and it is only just beginning to fade away) it was of a kind unmatched in the history of even religious controversy. Anecdotes, intended to undermine Newman's reputation, at one time formed the stock-in-trade of certain of his enemies; his personality, his style, his convictions, his dialectic, his character and fortunes have formed the subject of every sort of attack and innuendo and pedantic aspersion. His defects and his qualities, his limitations and his powers have been alternately exaggerated and depreciated to such an extent that the majority of men must find him a complete enigma. Here, however, we are concerned with his philosophical opinions alone, and our task will further be simplified if we arrange what we have to say under the names by which those who have written about him, as a philosopher, have attempted to describe him.

He has been described, then, as a sceptic, an empiricist, an intuitionist, an idealist, a traditionalist, and a mystic. Nobody who is well acquainted with the works of Cardinal Newman will deny that he himself would have protested against being placed in any such category and on one occasion and another he has defended himself, though not at any great length, against the charge of scepticism.

He had, at all times, an instinctive dislike for throwing men into this class or that as resulting, of necessity, in views shallow, incomplete and unjust: but the attempt to describe Newman himself in this manner has been singularly unfortunate. Such classing and defining has probably become inevitable in a day when there is so much to be read, and conscientious critics so seldom have time to read the books which they review, but it is strange, to say the least, that Newman should have been called an intuitionist after he had

denounced intuitionism and explained in the
" Grammar of Assent " why he was not an
intuitionist. Had he been, indeed, the architect
of some great system, or the author of any one
treatise strictly metaphysical, or a writer who
employed technical phrases and scientific method
it would have been no wonder that he should have
been thus peremptorily docketed and labelled and
set in his place; even though he had been writing
with the purpose of showing that philosophy had
nowhere reached so distinct a conclusion that a
clear minded man could sufficiently describe
himself or be sufficiently described in such terms
as those we have selected. But Newman's
writings were, as has already been said, " for the
most part occasional." Nothing was further from
his mind than the ambition to construct a system,
nor was his intellect of a nature which would have
excelled in such an undertaking. He had, in a
high degree, the peculiar insight of genius, and an
inexhaustible patience, subtlety and caution in the
expression of what men call its intuitions; and
it is no paradox to assert that he probably arrived
at something far more like a system than he, at
any time, consciously aimed at constructing,
partly from the very fact that he thus limited his
aspirations.

But a system he certainly did not construct:
and his clear apprehension of the fact that
philosophy is itself " on journey " and in a state of
transition: his continual insistance on the
impossibility of completing, at present, any

satisfactory basis in metaphysics or any basis that it would be wise to regard as *final*, afford a sufficient reason why it would seem premature to blame him (as he has been blamed) for not constructing a system which he gives reasons for considering it impossible at present to construct, or to set him down as belonging to some distinct school of philosophers when he has given reasons, which at least require an answer, why he considers it impossible at present to belong to any.

Nevertheless these names are not without their use as we shall probably see, for they will show us, taken one by one, what he was not, and will help, when taken together, to show us what he was.

He formed what will probably turn out to be a basis for a system and has given some sort of plan for a route in a new region of philosophy. He was the last of one order of minds and the first of another.   He cast aside, late in life, the whole set of statical arguments in which he had been brought up and fought his way to that dynamic conception of truth which has caused so much terror to the orthodox, not only in religion, but in every department of thought.   He entered boldly into the stronghold of subjectivism in philosophy, but found nothing to discourage him in the fact that truth is not something " abstract and detached," but lies, as it were, in the bosom of Humanity, " clinging to her and lost in her embrace."

But this is to anticipate and to express loosely what must be shown hereafter.

At present, I am but attempting such a general description of his position and the peculiar character of his mind as will form an introduction to a more exact and accurate account of his opinions than that which has been commonly given.

What it is necessary to keep before us, then, if we desire to be fair in our interpretation, is that he was ever concerned in direct and immediate matter of controversy: that he was as keen in dialectic as he was sympathetic and imaginative in character: that it was his habit in dispute to grant to his adversary all that his adversary required, for the sake of argument. He therefore frequently starts with supposing that all that scepticism begins with demanding may be granted and all that empiricism requires may be allowed; and yet insists that still there remains as good an argument for man's belonging to, and making himself one with the religious process, (which is, if you will, but a huge experiment made by humanity) as for his belonging to and making himself one with the ethical process—because he will find it as difficult to make a start for himself and keep outside them, as he would to jump out of the cosmic process— whence alone the others are assumed to have arisen, and parts of which they must therefore remain. "Newman sets authority," says Dr. Fairbairn, "where Hume sets association, and the rest of his theory of life is simply Hume's." Newman, however, is but demanding, as necessary to his argument, the admission of two facts, (1) that a religious element in humanity there is, though men differ in describing its nature, and (2) that the only test of its actual existence and of its being an objective fact in humanity is the test which Kant and Comte alike apply universally, namely, the testimony of the human race, or the largest number of men we can consult. If we have a sound ringing in our ears, in order to find out whether the ringing exists objectively, we ask somebody else; and if he says he hears it too, we think we are probably right in supposing the sound to be outside and not only within the ear; and if we suspect him, we ask others. This is all the objectivity we at first can attain : this is the first objectivity possible to man, though the object thus gained still lies within the consciousness of humanity. So also in religion, what Dr. Fairbairn calls Newman's " authority " is but this " objectivizing " of religion so far as is possible in the nature of things, and so far as essential to the continued existence of any thought or conduct at all.

This pecularity in his method, resulting in a certain philosophic isolation : this cautions, tentative movement in the direction of a synthesis which he never completed, and this bold analysis and (as some thought) reckless destructiveness of arguments for religion which he believed to be incomplete or sophistical or false or unreal, were facts, incidental to his time and position, of which he had, in his own way, a sufficiently clear apprehension. And so it happened that in his "*Apologia*" he found it necessary to make a protest against those who, seeming to regard the Christian religion as if it were something which could be cut into squares, tabulated and stereotyped, would have had him rush into opposition to certain modern developments in science. He warned such persons that it would be far better and more in accordance with the dignity of religion to stand still: and that, as in the days of Moses, so now, it would be found that the Lord would fight for them.

It seemed to him very undignified for a Catholic to commit himself to the work of chasing what might turn out to be phantoms, and in behalf of some special objections to be devising some new theory which, before it was completed might have to give place to some newer theory still. . . . .

So, too, in speaking of the relations of science and religion, he had said that whereas science is, of necessity, precise and exact in its expression, religion, on the other hand, is often vague, always symbolic, never exhaustive of the subject of which it treats: and this from the very nature of the case and the insufficiency of language itself.

He considered, therefore, that, in an age of transition such as ours, it might often be our duty to destroy without hesitation or remorse what we had found to be false in logic or misleading; even though we could, on the other hand, but doubt-fully and tentatively adumbrate the whereabouts of what was true. And when he was himself engaged in an attack upon prejudice or bigotry or when he was attempting to expose the fallacy of arguments, used in support of propositions which he nevertheless believed to be true—arguments which assumed too much or which seemed unfair to those against whom they were directed—he by no means spared the guilty: he slashed and cut in pieces with a brilliancy and high spirit which gained for him, among some, the reputation of being a mere controversialist; while, on the other hand, in his " *Essay on Development* " and in the " *Grammar of Assent* " he does but give in outline—and that sometimes dim and indistinct—a theory whose consequences he leaves to the inference of the reader.

But such a criticism of him as that he was a mere controversialist, though, speaking of his writings as they stand he makes it himself, would be an error of the first magnitude, if it meant that his intelligence was capable of dialectic and nothing more.

Far otherwise! He turned to controversy because he was compelled to do so: he turned to controversy because he perceived, with a clearness which itself betokened powers beyond those of a mere dialectician, how long the struggle must be before constructive effort could be of any avail and that if he was to succeed at all in his ultimate intent, a whole campaign would be necessary in the country of his enemies. The error, then, that I shall attempt to expose is not that his controversial works were his best, for all his most serious writing is, in some sort, controversial: but the error which attributes this fact to the limitations of his intellect or the narrowness of his philosophy, and not rather to the exigencies of the times.

Man never knows how anthropomorphic he is, nor have Englishmen yet fully discovered how deep seated is their bias against Rome. When they have learnt it, they will cease to blame Newman for doing what they will then perceive to have been a work which could neither be hurried nor delayed.

In order to make clear the position which Newman adopted in philosophy, it may be well at once to sum up and describe in outline the general argument, which was, in his view, preliminary to all discussions concerning the relations of philosophy and religion; and it is impossible to do this more satisfactorily than in the form of an answer to the following questions.

" If," it has been said, " Cardinal Newman held—as every one must hold—that it is right reason which ultimately shows us that certain things are true and others false, how does he show what is right reason ? If he contends that human reason is always fallible and that there is " no criterion of truth beyond the witness borne to truth by the mind itself," how can he ascertain the validity of those processes of the reason which discriminate the true from the less true and from the false ? If he considers that conscience and reason have, in the concrete, " no necessary connection," how can he conceive them to imply a common

source, a common subject, and a common
goal ? If, in short, he admits the premises
of scepticism, how does he come to the
conclusions of faith : and if he allows, as he seems
to have done, that the conclusion he deduces is
but a hypothesis, how does he lead us to act upon
it as certain ?"

Now much of the misapprehension disclosed
in these questions has arisen from a false interpretation of the terms which Newman commonly
employs. He uses the word "reason," for instance, as it was usually employed in his earlier
years as meaning simply "the reasoning faculty,"
the faculty which deduces from premises. Those
who use the word "reason" as meaning "the
whole man" in the sense in which Plato says "we
must make for the truth with the whole man," or,
again, those who use "reason" as distinguished
from the understanding, have often argued as if
Newman denied, that man taken as a whole, or
reason taken in this larger sense, could ever arrive
at a religion. Hence such persons accuse Newman
of falling into a dualism with an "impotent, instrumental reason" on one hand and "an authoritative conscience on the other." But there is no
more dualism in this conception than there is in
the fact that the premises in a particular syllogism
may be given, not by the special faculty which
syllogizes, but by the memory alone. No one
denies that there is a sense in which we may
speak of the mathematical powers or the power of
ratiocination as each of them implying a special

faculty, nor does Newman deny, on the contrary
he contends, that such a faculty can only be
rightly used when it is regarded as but one
" aspect " among others of our manifold nature
and our actual method of reaching conclusions.
The faculties must be separated in order that we
may define their special functions, but by that
very definition, we discover that they are essentially inherent in man as one continuous whole,
and, therefore, dependent on each other. Now it
is the attempt to separate the reason from the
religious or moral element in man which Newman
condemns throughout his sermon on " Faith as
contrasted with Bigotry." If in the " Grammar
of Assent " he appears to keep the faculties apart
it is from that ever increasing analytical tendency
to which I have already referred : but it does not
follow that he fell into the dualism of which he is
accused; nay, the aim of his writing is, from the
first, precisely the opposite—namely, to show that
the two elements in man are so essentially necessary to each other that they may rather be regarded
as the aspects of one than as separate powers at all.
The misapprehension is, however, a natural one,
and it arises from the fact that Newman was using
the words of opponents who divide some powers
and deny the existence of others—whose reality
can only be proved by analysis—while the part of
his writings in which he is saying what is peculiar
to himself, and not anticipating the objections of
his opponents is that in which he shows that
" philosophy " *can have no meaning and could*

not exist apart from the nature of man which is its
subject." (Sermon on Faith as contrasted with
Bigotry), etc., etc. All he begins by requiring is
that it should be man's whole nature, and not only
a part of it, which is studied.

Again, in speaking of the religious element in
man Newman sometimes speaks of it as conscience, sometimes as the religious sense, and
those who, for this reason, accuse him of begging
the question, accustomed to read only small
extracts from his works in which these expressions
occur, do not understand what his argument is.
From this misapprehension alone two opposite
accusations have arisen : those scholastics, who
have read the passages in which he explains that
he is not dealing with conscience " *in fieri* " but
simply " *de facto esse*," and that he is using the
word "conscience," not as implying what he
wants to prove, but as having reference to something which mankind have found it necessary to
describe by a separate name, accuse him of falling
into subjective scepticism.

That school of writers against religions of all
kinds who sometimes speak as if the whole religious view of things (wherever found) had not
grown up out of human nature, but had come
from some unknown source, whose existence they,
nevertheless, totally deny, find in the use of any
separate word for the religious element in man a
" *petitio principii*."

Now the explanation is not very far to seek.
Newman did not indeed divide the history of

mankind, neatly and conveniently into those periods, the theological, the metaphysical and the positive: but he did divide it into periods in which one of those elements (always present in man) becomes, of necessity, the predominant one. The religious element in the history of man is the primary element and first also in order of time: and this because "the sense of the whole comes first," nor have we a scientific or a logical right to displace such words as "conscience" (so long as they are used strictly within terms of experience and not made to imply an intuition, a power of seeing through phenomena), until we have found a scientific definition which is their real equivalent and really accounts for the whole of the religious or moral notions conveyed by such terms. That we never can do so completely follows from the fact (if it be a fact) that man will always be not only a metaphysical and scientific animal but a progressively religious animal: and such a writer as Comte not only allows that it is a fact but took it as his motto, "that man tends to become ever more and more religious."

There is then, one set of philosophers who would cut off religion altogether as something whose purpose is fulfilled and whose work is done.

There is another class of philosophers (often the very leaders whom the first class pretend to follow) who say that man is a permanently religious animal, and contend that religion is a permanent element in man, but reject it as it, in fact, exists, reject all its developments in man;

refuse to accompany its advance and look for it in the clouds or in themselves.

And there is a third class, who, with Newman, contend that if we perceive religion to be an element in ourselves, we must objectivise that element: if we acknowledge that it is an element in society, at large, and in humanity, we have no more valid reason to stand outside of it and to refuse to take our part in it, *whether by defending it or by improving it:* we have no more valid reason for considering ourselves simply superior to it, for refusing to act as from within it and insisting on acting as from above it, than we have to assume ourselves to be superior to humanity itself. The process of religious development in humanity requires the analytical mind and the synthetical mind as much as any other process: and to abandon to one set of minds alone so important a part of the life of humanity: or to act towards it the part, not of a friendly reformer or an ardent protector, but a contemptuous, bitter, irreconciliable foe—however great the temporary excuse—is an evil not only relatively to religion, but to humanity. For it is causing dissensions worse than civil wars: it assumes the great religious process to be founded in illusion and the cosmic process to be simply irreconcilable, ultimately as well as now, with the ethical. And yet the very men who take up this position are sometimes the boldest in affirming that the ethical process and the religious process are but aspects and results of the cosmic process itself.

That very often religious bodies appear to tolerate within them only a certain class of minds, while the very notion of reform is scouted as impertinence, is undoubtedly true. The blame of heresy does not always attach to him who is called a heretic: it rises frequently from the misrepresentation and tyranny of those who seize a position in a religious body for which they are intellectually incompetent. But how far such a state of affairs excuses, how far it justifies, how far it necessitates a protest against the whole religious idea, its institution, its organizations, its character, its influence and its destiny, common sense will inform us at once, if we do but compare our conduct in such a case as this with the conduct which we should hold towards the country to which we belong, or the State in which we are units. To destroy, instead of modifying, any characteristic development in authority or representation, can never be the action of true statesmanship. It were as wise to begin the sum by blotting out the figures.

There is a famous argument of Pascal's addressed to a sceptic, which illustrates so clearly the position of Newman that I shall find it useful here to quote it, and to explain what I consider its real meaning. Most men have found that they are bound to make certain positive assumptions in moral and social life, if they are to govern or to act, or, indeed, to live at all. By an inevitable sequence of events, he that attempts to stand in the way of the ethical process (as rushing forth to the fulfilment of its destiny in human society) finds that he soon comes into contact with the cosmic process, too; and that, after all, will never do; for, do what he will, he cannot jump out of that except by ceasing to live.

" To act we must assume and that assumption is faith," says Newman. And for any modern philosopher, who admits that to think is to act, and that to live (in the case of those properly called men) is to think, if what Newman says is true, then the following proposition is true likewise. " To live *we* must assume, and that assumption is faith." What have we to assume if we are to live? What do we assume (if we assume anything) in continuing to think, to act and to live? We assume that life is not an illusion. The very notion of final cause (however unscientifically it may have been treated) has arisen from this necessity of life, of act, of thought. In thinking for a moment we act for a future, which we assume, though it is a future which may never come. As long as we think, then, we must assume, nor can speculation set itself altogether outside the necessities which result from existing in time.

Let us now turn to Pascal's much-disputed argument with a sceptical friend. Keeping in mind the two questions:—(1) Do we practically assume life to be an illusion? (2) Have we a right speculatively to assume life to be an illusion? We shall probably see a meaning in Pascal's argument which its critics have not been accustomed to find there.

Pascal, then, argues that if there is a God, you suffer an infinite loss by not believing in Him. If there is not a God, but you believe that there is, you lose nothing. " Wager, then, that he exists!" he cries, " for you cannot sit aside, in this game, and refuse to play. You must wager one way or the other."

Voltaire replies that he does not see the necessity, and Matthew Arnold says contemptuously: " Did ever great reasoner reason so wildly?" And the argument appears at first flippant and inconclusive enough. " Wager that God exists!" The demand seems a little unscrupulous: and in using so soon the word " God " Pascal is perhaps speaking a little loosely.

But his meaning, if we take his argument as a whole, may perhaps be this :—" Assume that life is an illusion and you suffer an infinite loss: if it turns out, after all, that life can be made a reality. Assume that an illusion life is not, and you may make it a reality, while it is certain you can suffer no loss."

Nor is this all. You cannot stand aside from life and view it as a whole. This is a game in which all must play, or if they choose not to play it, the only alternative is to take away also the power to judge of it, for not to play this game at all is simply not to live.

If, then, you cannot stand aside and watch the game in such a sense as to be able to judge whether it is an illusion or not, what logical right have you to assume that an illusion it is? We only know anything to be an illusion by comparing it with reality. But our life and what is within it is all that we know. To take from the midst of life, then, what we call an illusion and then call the whole of life an illusion, to take from the midst of life what we recognize as a jest, and then call life itself a jest, is but to play with words. Nor have we a right to say that life as a whole may or may not be an illusion, for such a condition of mind assumes a point of view of which we are incapable, inasmuch as we have no right to assume, to begin with, a reality more real than the only thing we know. Assume, then, that an illusion life is not! Throw yourself into it and into all the great processes of life, political, religious, scientific, as having a goal which makes worth while the process! Nobody denies that the state of doubt is thinkable: not the greatest dogmatist on earth denies that ultimate inconclusiveness is a conceivable state of mind: but, if you have no right to assume that your own life is an illusion, a life which is but a point in the great process of things, much less right have you to assume that the great processes in which you find yourself are simply illusory, or have no end that is answerable to their activity, or a sufficiency in themselves. So, therefore, Pascal goes on to argue that though you begin by imagining the religion in which you find yourself stupid and absurd, yet " be stupid, take holy water," accus-

tom yourself to the point of view, throw yourself
into it. For in so doing, he means, you put yourself into the same sort of relation to the race of
which you form a part as you find yourself to
be in, of necessity, towards the great order and
process of the world of which you form a part;
and to assume it to be " stupid " is as inexcusable
as to assume yourself to be a judge in a matter of
experience, before you have entered into experience at all. This is a preliminary argument for
religion in general—and applies to any one form
of religion until we have come into contact with
some other. It is an external argument, and the
mistake about it has been the supposition that it
is a substitute for the internal arguments. Now
let us sum up Newman's argument on the same
subject and consider whether the two do not
supplement and explain each other.

First, then, he attempted to show that there
was nothing wonderful in the fact that in religion
we must begin with assumption, for in every
department of life—religious, social and moral—
we are equally bound to assume, nay in living at
all we may be said, in a certain sense, to start with
an hypothesis. And, though these assumptions
may rightly enough be described as hypotheses
looked at analytically, yet we are justified in
acting upon them as synthetically certain : for, as
we are justified in acting morally on the assumption that our fellow-men have an existence independent of our own (though this too is a point
which it may be beyond our powers to prove) so

are we justified in acting religiously in accordance
with the religious element in life—at what point
soever we come into contact with it—because that
religious element has a positive, undeniable
existence, and those who act as if it had no
separate existence or could be resolved, straight
off, into emotions which required no separate
treatment, are ignoring a fact in human nature.

We act in general and we reason in general,
for immediate and necessary purposes, in a similar
manner and on reasons which, at first, may
appear as little satisfactory or profound. What
we commonly call the " knowledge " conveyed to
us through our physical senses or brought to us
by social, moral and religious media, though it is
" defective "—(inasmuch as it lies within a certain
defined sphere)—nevertheless is reckoned by us as
enough, for the simple reason that " we have no
more." For the only antecedent presumption or
criterion of the truth of any theory or hypothesis
which regards man and his affairs is, in the words
of Burke, its suitableness to the *whole nature* of
man, and his nature as modified by his habits:
and we are thrown upon this because the universe
offers us no other. Accordingly, Newman insists
that true Catholicity is founded in the system of
nature and is characterized by its answering to, or
allowing for whatever may be shown, now or in
the future, to be its *needs* or its *powers*.

It is a mark, then, rather of bigotry than of
scepticism, he contends, to leave out of account the
religious element in life; as, on the other hand, it

is a márk of bigotry rather than religiousness to
pretend to find a purely speculative argument—
apart from the actual religious element in man—
for religion : as if philosophy could exist apart
from the nature of man which is its subject.
(University Sermons.)

Among other proofs of the existence of a
necessary religious element in man, one may be
found in the arguments which have been used to
throw doubt upon the ethical dictates of his
"moral sense," because those who doubt its
ethical trustworthiness do not question the fact that
such dictates there are, but force upon us the
inference that what is commonly called
"conscience" implies "primarily a religious
notion and only in the second place an ethical "—
that is, it begins with the sense of law and only,
at last, finds out what the laws are.

So, then, the dictates of such a supposed law
and the "principles of faith " are axioms of action
before they can be regarded as axioms of truth
(Tamworth Read : Room): but the life of man
being a series of acts, and thought itself being, in
a real sense, action, such axioms are justly
regarded as *true*, for truth is not to be sought as
something isolated and apart from the life of man,
but as lying within it—one with it and lost in it
and only to be found in it.

And thus we come at last to the great test of
religious truth, which, in his theory on Development, Newman elaborated in a manner so
strangely accurate as to have surprised both its

E

scientific and its historical critics, namely, the
vitality consequent on its answering in every
generation to the necessities of man. The existence of this vitality becomes historically a test and,
in the final resort, the only test, of religious
truth : in spite of the fact, considered side by side
with the test of development, that mere popularity
or " acceptance with the multitude " is sometimes
a sign of falsehood or corruption. And of this
vitality and its real value the only test is its steady
growth or development—*i.e.*, its movement in one
direction rather than another—its consistent
advance; its constant survival in spite of attacks;
*its power to assimilate from what is without; in
short all the tests of growth which can be applied
to an organism.* Of this religious element in man
the Catholic Church claims to be the natural
medium—the only possible protectress and guar-
dian; in every age relating its past to the present
and the present to the future, mediating, as it
were, between the last man in humanity and the
first, so as to curb the self-sufficiency of the one
and modify the superstition of the other, " in
accordance with the advance of the scientific
temper."

In short, taking the works of Cardinal
Newman in their result (whatever they may prove
and whatever they may not succeed in proving)
they seem, at any rate, to show in this preliminary argument for the reasonableness of religion,
that, as there is an ethical and a cosmic process
going on in the world, so also there is a religious,

and that the last is the necessary medium of adjustment between the other two, as well as their inevitable corrective and restraint.

In what manner these three are one and in what manner it is true to say that the cosmic process can be modified by the other two, and, again, in what sense, and on what authority, the Church has been able to make this claim and act upon it—all these questions are proposed and discussed by Newman in his study of the Church as an organism. If it lives at all it lives because it has been able to select and reject, with the relative infallibility of other organisms, what is food for it and what is poison.

(1) NEWMAN AS SCEPTIC AND IDEALIST.

It may seem to some a strange and difficult fact that two great apologists such as Pascal and Newman should each in his own way have been characterised by that sad earnestness and almost wistfulness which gives to their writings a peculiar undertone of gravity and pathos. It seems as if the question to which Butler could attempt no reply—the question in its own nature unanswerable why so frail a creature as man should be set in the midst of so many and so grievous sorrows and temptations, were ever ringing in their ears.

They would not be satisfied with the easy solutions of " an ideal optimism," or cover up the sacred mystery of life with the verbiage of dogmatists. Both of them, therefore, dwelt as men apart : as men who have seen some vision, or as strangers from some far city. They dwelt among men, but with another destiny, and their gaze was set upon the term of a solitary journey.

For each of them seems, in his own time, a solitary figure :—Pascal, wandering with pensive tread from church to church in the older streets of Paris, and Newman, in his latter years, as one who sits in some darkened theatre alone, watching with intent and wistful eyes, while, in long procession, there pass before him " all the days of the years of his pilgrimage."

Nor should it be astonishing if shallow and complacent minds or little, hurried souls—who have never learned to look into the face of life— have been impatient of this tone of sadness and this isolation of thought, and imputed them to some hidden scepticism or morbid credulity or to both.

Thus it happened that the versatile Brougham and that master of persiflage, Voltaire, could impute Pascal's piety, its intensity and earnestness, to the sad effects of that accident—one of the miracles of materialism—which has played so large a part in the literature of sceptical flippancy.

Nor have the lesser wits of neo-scholasticism failed to contribute their quota of contemptuous criticism to the restless hubbub of censure poured forth from every direction by all sorts and conditions of men—those who despair of philosophy and those who believe in a philosophy mechanically complete but completely empty, alike join in the condemnation of writers who were neither school-men in philosophy nor sceptics in religion. " Alas !" they cry, " that men of such capacity should have wasted their lives in attempting the solution of problems which are insoluble. Why did they not rather turn their attention to social questions, to politics, to scientific research ? Or, at any rate, if they must have written about philosophy, why did they not give themselves to some system—neat and rounded off—such as can be readily described in a Dictionary of Biography, and such as we find in the text books of the schools? Such a course would have acted as a tonic, pulled them together, and made men of them. Instead of which they must ever keep returning to questions of whence and whither—' the greatness and misery of man ' —topics which have busied the wisest heads in humanity for ages, but have never yet received satisfactory treatment or given birth to a tolerable hypothesis !"

Among the mob of pedants, on one side, and practical men on the other, it has become the fashion to charge both Pascal and Newman with a fatal incoherence and inconsistency of thought, and, hence there has arisen an attempt to sub·stantiate the charge of scepticism and credulity against them both. And indeed the charge of scepticism as it has been preferred against Newman is, in some cases, of a precisely similar nature to that which has been preferred against Pascal. For Newman, like Pascal, was not satisfied with making a general and easy admission—such as we read at the beginning of text books in Philosophy—that scepticism cannot be refuted on its own grounds; he pursued and described the consequences of this admission: he attempted to show that it involves a fact in the constitution of man's mind and therefore sets a necessary limit to his thought, not in one question

alone, but in all questions in which we desire
finality or look for some absolute reply. And it is
from the proof of these limitations themselves that
both Pascal and Newman have drawn one of their
proofs for the necessity of religion, a necessity
which is therefore no mere exaggeration of the
significance of man's religious aspirations, but a
necessity inherent in the very nature of man and
such that it is impossible for him ever to be rid
of it.

It is not, therefore, altogether consistent in
teachers of neo-scholasticism, to consider Newman
a sceptic because he admits in particulars what
every philosopher has admitted in general; nor,
on the other hand, is it permissible to consider
Newman credulous, because after he has completed the argument by which he attained the
religious position he ultimately held, he can look
back over the process and history of religious
faith in the minds of men and find there vague
tokens as of some Divine purpose or marks as of
some but half-revealed design. In these conclusions he may use the poetry of religion or the
rhetoric of the Fathers of the Church; but the
conclusion he reached he founded on scientific and
philosophical grounds.

The argument must be answered first or the
conclusion shown to reach too far before his
enemies have a right to claim that his faith had
become credulity or his idealism merely mystical.

(1) It has been said of Pascal's defence of
Christianity that he makes it all to turn on the

literal truth of the story of the fall, and that, inasmuch as modern criticism cannot receive that story, his argument must perish with it.   But there could not be a misrepresentation more complete. With whom, then, is Pascal supposed to be arguing? With men who already believed in the fall? No, for he is addressing those who do not even believe in a God.   All that Pascal attempts is to show that man's greatness and his misery point to a fact which may be summed up in a conception like that conveyed in the history of the Fall. He makes use, that is, of an argu-ment for accepting the history of the Fall and considering it as a dogmatic fact. And then he proceeds to show that for man, in the condition thus described, Christianity is so completely the sort of remedy required that we may, without violence, assume it to be the true one—in spite of the difficulties which it suggests, the questions it fails to answer, the mysteries which it proposes to our faith.

Here Pascal, like Newman, is using the language of complete argument and the language of ordinary Christians. But to assume him to be a historical dogmatist, to be taking the story of the Fall as crudely and literally true, is as little just as it would be to assume that he is a specu-lative dogmatist because he found reason for believing the dogmas of the Catholic Church. All men know, on the contrary, that the reasons which he found were not those of the dogmatists in philosophy, to whom he is as often opposed as he is to the sceptics. The dogmas of the church were to Pascal what they were to Newman—the inevitable language of religion, often vague, always symbolic, never exhaustive of the subject of which they treat; but the exactest expression possible to man, in his changing existence, of the sure and certain hope that lay within him—ever growing more consistent and mature. It was the actual state of man, then, which he found described in the Fall—not so much the historical event which accounts for it; and the dogma, involved in the conception of the Fall, shows, in his mind, that the Christian and Jewish religions had adequately diagnosed and truly appreciated that disease of human nature which it calls " sin." That the closeness of the fact to the account so given of it proves some such fact as the Fall to be true; that it proves " original sin " to represent a fact, he certainly contends: not, that the Fall took place in a certain manner, time and place. His argument, therefore, stands, without the necessity of introducing an historical dogmatism, foreign to Pascal's nature and mode of thought and plausibly imputed rather on account of the fragmentary nature of his writing than from a careful consideration of his method. Nor is it only his clear apprehension of the fact that " nature itself is, perhaps, but a first habit," the only point where so wooden an interpretation of his argument would seem to break down, for his thesis —so clear to those familiar with his writings— proves at last to be, not, as superficial expressions

sometimes seem to indicate, the supernatural value
of Christianity (though that he believed) but the
depth of it—the fact that it touches human nature
at its base. This, for him, came at last to constitute, rather than to prove, the supernatural value
of Christianity.

(2) I have described this misapprehension of
Pascal's argument on the Fall in order to shed
some light on what I conceive to have been the
manner in which Pascal and Newman alike
regarded dogma. It is ever to them symbolic, and
not to be taken as crude, literal fact even when, as
in the case of the Fall, they themselves, no doubt,
took the fact as historical. The confusion which
attributes to Pascal an argument entirely hinging
upon the Fall as an historical fact has, however,
a long history, and may be said to have attached
to Christianity, in some sense or other, even since
it began to exist—and the confusion is owing to an
apparent ambiguity in the method of great
Christian writers themselves.

" St. Augustine, from the very richness of his
great nature," says Harnack, " while he attacked
the Biblicists with Tertullian and set the creed
above the Bible, yet could not rid himself of the
notion that, in the Bible, every word is
revelation."

In like manner Pascal and Newman are afraid
suddenly to let drop a fixed historical conception,
though the arguments they use do, in fact, reach
below it and will stand without it.   And this

apparent inconsistency, for apparent rather than real it is, has not been altogether without its value. It has been a reasonable attitude toward the Bible to stand out against its disruption and the tendency to explain it away in accordance with every new theory in criticism, inasmuch as such interpretations have, again and again, turned out to be false; and, had they been used, the true meaning of the Bible (sometimes not historical at all, but an allegory, and sometimes strictly in accordance with the history known to Jews but conveying an impression completely false—if not corrected by other historical evidence)—would have been lost more completely and for a longer time than can now be the case. What is truly deplorable is an attitude for which Newman and Pascal are not responsible, the attitude of contempt towards inductive criticism, a sort of labour which Pascal commended as of great value, and in which Newman has himself, in some degree, taken part. But such an attitude as that I have drawn is, without doubt, the attitude of Pascal and of Newman towards actual doctrine, and it is this attitude which has so widely created the tradition that Newman was both sceptical and credulous and suffered from a consequent incoherency which he never fully faced.

And as St. Augustine is the explanation, to some extent, of a common error, so is he the explanation of the deeper source of that error, namely, the notion that Newman and Pascal were altogether sceptics, philosophically. In this sense

they were, that is, they could admit the whole
case for scepticism and yet believe.

" Not unfamiliar," says Harnack, " with the
realm of knowledge of the objective world, St.
Augustine yet wished to know but two things,
God and the *soul;* for his scepticism had dissolved the world of external phenomena, but in
the flight of these phenomena the facts of the
inner life had, after painful struggles, remained
to him as *facts*.   Even if there exists no evil and
no God, there still exists unquestionably the fear
of evil.   Out of this, i.e., through psychological
analysis, one can find the soul and God and
sketch a picture of the world.   Hence the sceptic
can arrive at the knowledge of truth, for which
the marrow of the soul cries."

These words may be used with almost equal
truth of Pascal and Newman, if we do but add the
explanation which arises out of the exigencies of
controversy with Jesuits, Protestants and readers
of Montaigne in France, with disciples of Hume
and the sceptics of the 18th century in England.

(3) With regard to the sense in which
Newman has been considered a sceptic, and the
manner in which this view of him has arisen,
something ought to be said, because here, too, an
ambiguity has arisen which ought not to exist.
The word sceptic is popularly supposed to mean
one who does not believe in the popular religion.
It is also supposed to mean one who has no
philosophical principles at all.   In these senses

very few would be inclined to call Newman a sceptic.

But the meaning which is given to the word by philosophers is very different. Thus certain dogmatic philosophers call idealists (whether objective or subjectivè) sceptical, because it is supposed that all those, who disbelieve in the ordinary doctrines about matter, question the veracity of the senses. Such a use of the word is misleading because Idealists of every description are just as ready as anyone else to trust the senses, in their own sphere. They only deny that they can be trusted in another sphere than their own or that they can solve a problem which is concerned with that upon which the senses themselves are dependent, namely, in what manner it may be said that material objects exist, whether " per se " or " a se," etc. Those, too, have been called sceptics who doubt the objective reality of space, motion and time, and this from a similar confusion of mind.

So, again, there are those who consider there is something sceptical in the avowal that the mind has no criterion of truth beyond the witness borne to truth by the mind itself. And in all these senses Newman was liable to the charge of scepticism, though, as all men know, he objected to the name as misleading—and that even in his limited philosophical sense—as applied to St. Augustine, Pascal or himself. The attempt to confuse the two meanings and then apply them to him, in order to create a prejudice against him as not believing in religion, would constitute what theologians call "grave matter," for it would amount to slander, but it is doubtful whether any such attempt has been made altogether consciously. The confusion of men's minds on these subjects is all but universal and will account for much which Newman himself believed to be malignant misrepresentation, though it is to be feared that this stupidity has now and then been found exceedingly convenient.

From the very first, then, and even as a boy, Newman tells us, in the "Apologia," he held the unreality of material phenomena. Later on he made the usual distinction between matter and its phenomena and, at last, began a line of thought which ceases to look out for a reality wholly *behind* phenomena, but finds in phenomena the sacrament of reality and all that is possible to thought within the ever widening consciousness of man—in the past as experienced, in the present as experience, in the future as being the completed idea to which these tend. But this view of things he hinted at rather than explained and was slowly approaching when he wrote the book on "Development." The difficulties in which he was placed by the teaching of the schools threw him back and he was obliged to go over familiar ground, once more, in the "Grammar of Assent" without ever completing the conception of truth which he had started so early.

He does not, he says, disbelieve in eternal truths, but does not see how men in general are to be made to act on them so as consciously to realise them.   He sees that it is eternal truths which necessarily make themselves a place, throw men into societies, create the organisms by which they become known, develop and thus survive, while error, of its own nature, decays inasmuch as those eternal truths are the reality by which man lives and in accordance with his growing knowledge of which he grows.   Nevertheless, it remains true that men see these things as " afar off " and need to have them " in their heart and in their mind," —if " the Kingdom of God is to be within them.

Again, in a pamphlet which he published in 1838 the fundamental idea, he says, is consonant to that to which he had been so long attached : " It was the denial of the existence of space except as a subjective idea of our own minds."   Again, taking the demonstrated fact that the earth moves round the sun and the opposed notion that the sun moves round the earth—he says, " If our idea of motion be but an accidental result of our present senses neither proposition is true and both are true : neither true philosophically, both true for certain practical purposes in the system in which they are respectively found : and physical science will have no better meaning when it says that the earth moves than plane astronomy when it says that the earth is still."

In like manner, the words which we mentioned above, denying that the mind can gain any criterion of truth beyond the witness borne to truth

by the mind itself, are to be found in the
" Grammar of Assent."

And the words " Bigotry is distinguished
from faith in that it presumes beyond the proper
ground of religion. It persists not in abandoning
argument, but in arguing only in one way.   It
takes up not a religious but a philosophical position—" have been taken to mean, not that
religion is something *sui generis* and has its own
evidence and its own mode of growth, development and life, but that we must have recourse to
faith in such a manner as to do without any kind
of argument at all.

In like manner the following words have been
misrepresented as meaning that the intellect has
nothing to do with religion. " No one can deny
to the intellect," he says in the University
Sermons, " its own excellence or deprive it of its
due honours; the question is merely this, whether
it be not limited in its turn as regards its range,
so as not without intrusion to exercise itself as
an independent authority in the field of morals and
religion."

Here he is speaking of that Liberalistic and
Benthamite mode of using the reason, which, with
a perfectly logical method, but on the assumption
that nothing vague or incomplete or inchoate can
be regarded as, in any sense, true, empties morals
and religion of their content and calls such a
procedure progressive. As the object of the intellect is truth and that object is considered by such
persons to belong to the intellect exclusively—they

have considered that Newman here implies that moral and religious truth as such is unattainable and consequently that these words contain an avowal of philosophic scepticism.

Goethe, who was but little in sympathy with the strident Liberalism of his day, saw how important it is to regard the religious element in man as something sacred—as a sense of the fitness of things, as a sense of what true culture consists in, as a sense of man's true relation to the universe. All men know what he said of its conception of purity and its view of marriage as a sacrament— they are triumphs of the religious sense for the general culture of mankind.   And on what are really similar grounds, " proofs of religion," " *from evidences*," Newman pronounces " to some extent a usurpation of the reason, the reason taking the place of the religious sense."   Nevertheless, he will not allow the religious sense to be regarded as an intuition carrying us beyond the bounds of experience, nay, it is in its nature weaker than the senses generally so called " in proportion to the excellence of the good it confers."   It is, however, an element in the history of man—distinct—*sui generis*—and must, at last, be tested as all other elements in man are tested, by its general efficacy in the development of man himself.   And lest the impossibility of gaining any stronger foothold than this should seem to lead us to a barren and dreary scepticism, he says—" If our senses support the media by which we are brought together and hold intercourse with one another,

F

are disciplined and enabled to benefit others—it is enough."

Such a remark has been considered—when added to his peremptory rejection of intuitionism —to land us in pure positivism—as making the ultimate appeal to the religious and social element in man each in its own sphere,—and finding the proof for such objectivity as is required simply in the consent of large masses of men in the history of the world. "It may be that the dogmas we have are the best representations of truth"—the best possible, he means, to man in his present stage of development, and therefore not to be destroyed, but interpreted, and the meaning implicit in them developed. "The knowledge belonging to the religious sense, though defective, is not insufficient for the purpose for which it uses it—for the plain reason that it has no more." And yet even this knowledge is itself but inchoate. It is employed on things scarcely within the proper range of evidence. "Philosophy," he says, "is reason exercised upon knowledge."

"But," on the other hand, "faith cannot be called knowledge," for "we are commonly supposed to *know* things when we have ascertained them by the natural methods for ascertaining them, viz.:—by means of evidence, but faith proceeds far more on antecedent grounds than on evidence." "Reason is instrumental and faith creative"—but the informations of faith have not as they stand become what we commonly call knowledge.

Reason then, he seems to say, depends for a right conclusion on right premises and strict logic, but what in this complicated scene of falsehood and truth, right and wrong, is to supply us with right premises? Nay—who is to say what is the right use of reason? Out of the thousand paths that run into the darkness from beneath our feet who is to set us in the right one or warn us against the wrong?

And thus, like St. Augustine, having dissolved the world of external phenomena, he turns, like St. Augustine, to other difficulties presented by the arguments for the existence of God.

" Such works on Natural Theology as treat of marks of design in the creation which are beautiful and interesting to a believer in God " are often, " when men have not recognised the voice of God within them,   ineffective,   and this moreover possibly from some unsoundness in the intellectual basis of the argument."   " Evidences," he observes, " often do little to turn man to a religious life."   For God, in an argument for His existence, as Hegel says, must be Himself the absolute ground for the initial step.

On this passage Cardinal Newman has written a note to the effect that the argument from order with which he deals in the " Grammar of Assent " does not suffer from the same kind of unsoundness or fall with the argument from design : but we are here concerned with what he considered that unsoundness to be, and this we shall be able to gather from the following quotation out of his

letter on the " Tamworth Reading Room." Here
too he came, later on to consider his language too
absolute : but for our present purpose it is enough
to take the words as they stand—premising only
that they are used in direct controversy with the
sceptical or half sceptical thought of his day :—

"The whole framework of nature is con-
fessedly a tissue of antecedents and consequents :
we may refer all things forwards to design or back-
wards on a physical cause. La Place is considered
to have had a formula which solved all the motions
of the solar system : shall we say that those
motions came from this formula or from a Divine
Fiat? Shall we have recourse for our theory to
physics or to theology? Shall we assume matter
and its necessary properties to be eternal or mind
with its Divine attributes? . . . . . The one
hypothesis will solve the phenomena as well as the
other. Say not it is but a puzzle in the argument
and no one ever felt it in fact. So far from it, I
believe that the study of nature when religious
feeling is away, leads the mind, rightly or wrongly,
to acquiesce in the atheistic theory as the simplest
and easiest."

Again—a little further on in the same letter—
he adds :—" To those who are conscious of matter
but not conscious of mind, it seems more rational
to refer all things to one origin such as they know,
than to assume the existence of a second such as
they know not."

It has been commonly supposed that Newman
gets out of the difficulties here suggested by

inventing or discovering a religious intuition which pierces through phenomena and finds a Reality behind them—but that is in flat contradiction to his own words, which are as follows :—

After speaking of certain schools of thought in which it is maintained that certitude is simply and always a mistake, he continues :—" There are others who . . . . . in order to vindicate the certainty of our knowledge . . . . have recourse to the hypothesis of intuitions . . . . which belong to us by nature and may be considered to elevate our experience into something more than it is in itself " (" Grammar of Assent " —Chapter on the Illative sense.)

Dealing as he is with certitude—as it is in fact —and not attempting to justify it or deal with it " *in fieri*," he considers it enough to appeal to the fact that certitude is felt and to the common voice of mankind.

With the origin of the error that he makes an interior intuition the criterion of truth for every individual we shall deal later on. Here it is enough to say that his saying that the moral feelings and the religious feelings are *like intuitions*, and, in some, appear *as if* infallible instincts : his representation of the religious element in man as if a " sense " and the importance of its being so regarded : his representation of the moral element in man as if a " sense," and his insistence on the vagueness and wretched insufficiency of that element if it is not so educated as to be able to act as the senses do—to warn us from every taint in a poisonous atmosphere—this is what has no doubt led to the mistake. It is a mistake, however, which overthrows the whole structure of Newman's argument for religion from the base.

Others, again, have gone so far as to imagine that Newman makes certitude a criterion of truth, but in his book on the Development of Doctrine he represents the problem we start with as suggested by the fact that as soon as people begin to reason on morals and religion they come to different conclusions and arrive at opposite certitudes :

Again, in the " Grammar of Assent " he distinctly states that as certitudes may be opposed in different people certitude is not a final test of truth.

By this time our readers will probably understand how it was possible for Prof. Huxley to say that out of some of the works of Cardinal Newman he thought he could put together the best handbook of infidelity it was possible to recommend to the young student.

We are now, therefore, in a position to give in some detail the case (which we have already described in general) of those who thus regard his philosophical opinions.

"Here is a writer," they might say, "who suspects, and in some degree exposes the unsoundness of the argument from design : who tells us that conscience is no argument to those who distrust its informations : who denounces the feebleness of our reasoning faculty and proves it so

dependent upon its first movements and the premisses with which it may happen to be provided
that its conclusions in any individual instance may
seem to be a matter of chance: who not only
admits but takes pains to show that certitude is no
test of truth inasmuch as certitudes are often
opposed: who has exposed the absurdity of private
judgment or a reliance, consequently, upon our
reason, our instincts, our intuitions—as if they
were somehow inherently superior to other people's
just because, forsooth, they are our own—with a
sarcastic brilliance which has never been sur-
passed: who shows that the mind itself supplies
our sole criterion of truth and yet that, as our mind
cannot prove its own authority, it is as fallible a
criterion as any other; here is a writer who admits
or demonstrates all this in favour of scepticism and
yet, at the same time, demands that by a process of
reason and an act of judgment we shall confer a
sort of infallible authority upon conscience, implicitly obey our reason and set up our religious
instincts as an unerring guide—if we do but obey
them—perhaps to an infallible church, but certainly to a whole circle of moral and religious
truth !"

Such is the charge against Newman, and the
reader, from what we have already said, may, perhaps, be able to give an answer.

(2).—NEWMAN AS TRADITIONALIST.

The conception of Newman's dialectic which has resulted in the questions mentioned in the last chapter has been owing to a fact sufficiently clear to those who know what Newman's position was in Oxford when he began his attempt to make some standing room for the great sacramental system of Catholicism—as it is found, especially, in the works of Origen and Augustine. He was face to face with an opponent who not only rejected Catholicism, but ignored the significance of religion altogether. He found himself in the midst of a Liberalism at once sceptical and empirical.

With his main position drawn out and defended in the "History of the Arians," where he shows how he stands with regard to the philosophical Catholicism of the Fathers, he was compelled to build his outworks in the very midst of the enemy's country. He could not bring sceptic, empiricist, and utilitarian at once to the standpoint adopted by himself, nay, it is clear at once that he could do no more than describe his position as a hypothesis, though a hypothesis which man is practically bound, in some fashion, well or ill, to make.

He does not, then, begin with denouncing

scepticism as simply false and with a destructive attack upon the principles of empiricist and utilitarian. On the contrary, he shows he can grant their contention within a certain sphere; but he contends that, on their own principles, they must either go further or not so far: that they adopt narrow definitions of "knowledge," "expediency," and "utility," and then argue from the broader meaning which the rest of the world attaches to the words.

Grant, again, that the senses are what "sceptics" consider them: grant that we cannot prove the existence of an outer world—yet, still, we are compelled to act and we do act, in accordance with our senses, and as if an outer world existed. We trust our senses, therefore, in their own sphere. But if we trust our senses in their own sphere—may it not be shown that there is a sphere also for the religious element in man, and that we have the same kind of reason for believing in the existence of that as something *sui generis* and distinct and having a definite part to play in man's life, as we have for so taking the senses and the social and moral elements in man.

As we can act, and usually find ourselves compelled to act, in accordance with the premisses provided by what Hume calls "custom" in the case of the other elements in man, so we can consistently begin by acting in accordance with the premisses provided by "custom" (if such it be considered) in the case of the religious element in man. And as an object for the senses is provided

in the external world—(how little so ever the existence of it can be proved or made comprehensible)
—so an object for the religious element in man is
provided by the religious idea of God—incompre-
hensible, indeed, and in His own nature, as the
schoolmen speak, infinite *and with no real relation
to man*, but an object to which man, nevertheless,
has a relation, as towards the universe—the
relation established by the history of man's
experience, for the history of religion is but the
history of man's relation to all that he has ever
called God and worshipped.

Now, as we have had occasion to say before, a
great deal of confusion has arisen from Newman's
use of the word " reason " as describing a faculty
merely instrumental. He meant that the intellect
cannot be regarded as an entirely separate faculty
by means of which he can get at truth, because we
must make for the truth " with the whole man "—
" we must think," as a great French philosopher
has said, " with the very body."

Had " expediency " in the mouths of
utilitarians meant what it meant to Burke " what is
suitable to the whole man," and did experience
include all that Burke made it include—in the
historical attempt of man to discover what is suitable to him as a whole, and " if the greatest happiness of the greatest number " included a happiness
satisfying to the element in man, which holds
together and can look down upon the categories,
as well as the happiness acquired within the
categories (if we may so speak)—utilitarians and

empiricists might claim to be profound philosophers.

Newman, therefore, in his book on Development, attempts to bring together into one his
religious and philosophical teaching—the sacramental system of the Fathers and his philosophical
defence of religion against the sceptics and
empiricists of his day.   And the question which
lies at the bottom of his Essay on Development is
really this :—" How is it possible to ascertain, in
accordance with the process necessitated by the
ratiocinative faculty, what is the true object of the
religious element in man—whatever that element
may turn out to be?"   And it is from his answer
to this question that Newman has come to be
regarded as a Traditionalist in the same sense as
De Bonald or Lamennais—and an Empiricist in
the same sense as Hume.

For his answer practically amounts to this :
that the experience of the individual and the
experience of the race are the sole authorities to
which we can have recourse, whether in the case
of the physical senses or in the case of what have
been called the social sense, the moral sense, the
religious sense.   When we have no experience or
no sufficiently clear experience of our own we
must, in this matter, as in others, throw ourselves
back upon and ascertain (as far as possible) the
sum of the experience of the human race in that
subject which corresponds with the " sense " with
regard to which we start our enquiry.

Nor is this to deny, as Cardinal Newman is

careful to remark, that there are "eternal truths,"
ideas, realities ascertainable by man: it is only to
insist that the stubborn fact remains that no such
ideas have historically shown themselves sufficiently commanding to become the basis of public
union and action." They have been the reason
why men have acted together, but men have been
but half conscious of the reason. As man in
becoming conscious of himself gets to see how far
he can trust his senses, so Humanity becomes
conscious of itself through a Catholic organisation
—whether religious or not—and then proceeds to
discover what it really is which it trusts to in its
development, whether it has any faculty which it
can use on the journey it suddenly becomes aware
it has, for ages, been taking, whether, as an
organism it has the power of finding its way or
rejecting what is poison for it, assimilating what is
food in a similar manner to that in which an
individual may.

The religious element in man does not,
according to Newman, supply itself, as it were, by
means of an intuition with its own object. It is
but an unsatisfied craving: a sense of law, in
general, but no knowledge of the law; a sense of
right and wrong in general, but no knowledge
what is right and what is wrong; a sense of what
is permanent, what is real, what is universal, but
no knowledge how to express these things to itself.
It is dependent for its growth, energy, and the
exercise of its function, as the physical senses are,
upon something conceived as external to it, some-

thing brought to it from without. It is in need of
fertilization either by some sort of confirmation of
what its desires portend or by some actual object—
from a fetish to Spirit—which answers to them.
Self-fertilization seems impossible to it. Indeed,
did we not adopt the morality and religion, at least
provisionally, which we find around us, we should
but wear ourselves out in a perpetual round of
thought—starting at no beginning and resulting
in no conclusion.

With language, at any rate, begin we must,
and language is but a tradition we have received.

Thus, too, in the sphere of religion (which is
not infinite though it brings us into contact with
all human expressions for the infinite) we must
seek the object of religious aspiration—from
without.

In the case of our senses we are dependent
upon the sum of the experience of the human race
for their right education and continuance in
activity.   On the basis of experience alone (not
yet having reached a point where we can appeal to
anything else) it is from the race of which we form
a part that we receive not only our education, but
our life and our senses themselves. The physical
structure and conformation of our brain are as
truly a material tradition as language is a spiritual.
We cannot get outside the influence of tradition or
the necessity for authority by any act of the private
judgment, how bold soever, for the language in
which we think, the rules by which we argue and
the brain which is essential to our making any

movement in thought at all are material or spiritual traditions from the past, though they are in the very act of moving on towards a future.

Now it is the religious experience of mankind which provides this onward movement at once with a definite starting point and an object—ever approached, though never completely gained.

Were it not for the religious experience of others or the religious element in humanity taken as a whole, the indefinite aspirations of the individual would find no object at all—not even a fetish, but would exhaust his energies by their persistent recurrence, their incessant claim, their insatiable craving: for even a fetish cannot be worshipped till some evidence from without has confirmed the notion of divinity already vaguely present in the mind. Man's reason is defective because it is a part of a whole. It is so, when it does not realise its organic communion both with special faculties as memory or conscience or with the race. Man, by himself, would still be a religious animal, just as he would still be a laughing animal;—but, by himself, he would probably never laugh,—and, by himself, without the confirmation and encouragement supplied by the necessities of *thought-in-language*, he would probably never worship. In short, the individual finds the unity and the objective validity of thought by contact with other men. Such words are taken to imply that traditionalism which is condemned by the Church—just as the other half of

Newman's argument is taken to imply the intuitionism so condemned. But the traditionalism condemned by the Church was concerned with a primitive revelation and considered primitive revelation a substitute for metaphysical proof : and with primitive revelation and metaphysical proof this argument has, at this point, nothing to do. It does not deny : it does not affirm—anything with regard to subjects which could not be introduced, at this point, into Newman's argument—without begging the question. It does but prescind from them—until the argument, built on premisses which sceptics and empiricists may admit, is completed.

It denies, indeed, that any argument for the existence of God can be introduced before this argument is completed :—but it affirms that sceptic and empiricist, even if right as far as they go, are bound to admit the religious idea into their notion of experience and among the objects with which man's nature, taken as a whole, is concerned. We have no right to begin by cutting out of man what forms in him a characteristic element.

We depend, then, upon the traditions of the race to which we belong even in the most intimate acts of our mind.

And one of these traditions (whether we choose to consider it physical or not) has culminated or is expressed in the religious element in man.

To the sum of the religious experience of the human race (so far as we can ascertain it, even though we begin only with one other human being) must we go, for the witness we need and for the object of which we are in search—as we begin by getting somebody else to tell us whether they hear the distant cry we hear, or feel the vague aspirations we notice in ourselves. Whether this religious emotion is something characteristically human, or something simply abnormal to be destroyed as evil, and whether man has been able to supply it with a place, an object, a function in his life, and what that place, object or function may be, we can only find by consulting humanity itself in whatever manner we find it possible best to do so.

Prescinding, then, from metaphysical proof and primitive revelation, how shall we arrive at some notion of such *truth* in religion as shall satisfy our need? How is the religious element in man to be supplied with an object in such a manner as to satisfy the claims of his ratiocinative faculty?

Now truth, as we are here concerned with it, " is not something abstract and detached, but must lie in the bosom of humanity." It is the ultimate Reality of things in accordance with which things are rightly done and so, in the long run, succeed, or in contradiction to which things are wrongly done, and, in the long run, fail. " Morality is," in this sense, truly called " the nature of things."

As early as 1756 Burke published his ironical " Vindication of Natural Society." The reasoning, as is well known, was intended to show that "if the practice of all moral duties and the foundation of Society rested upon having their reasons made clear and demonstrative to every individual"—the world would fall into ruins.

"Show me," he says, "an absurdity in religion and I will undertake to show a hundred for one in political institutions."

"If after all you should confess all these things, yet plead the necessity of political institutions, I can argue perhaps with superior force concerning the necessity of artificial religion: and every step you advance in your argument you add a strength to mine." Here we have an argument for religion drawn from expediency.

In the "Apologia" Newman writes that one of the propositions of Liberalism which he earnestly denounced and abjured was that "utility and expedience are the measure of political duty."

Nevertheless, if we consider the speculative difficulty with regard to political institutions to be a *real one* and the necessity for religion to lie in the *reality of things* and substitute the words "naturally evolved" for the unhistorical word "artificial" applied to religion, the argument begins to have some resemblance to that which is used by Newman in his book on "Development."

It is founded, indeed, on expediency—but on a broad conception of expediency entirely different from that which Newman denounced and abjured. For expediency, regarded as it would then be regarded, becomes a test of truth—if truth is taken as that reality which lies in the nature of things

G

and is ever attempting to express itself more and more completely.

For what is, in fact, Burke's conception of expedience? "Expedience," says Burke, in another place, "is that which is good for the community and good for every individual in it. Now this expedience is the desideratum to be sought either without the experience of means or with that experience. . ."

But "one of the ways of discovering a false theory is comparing it with practice. This is the true touch-stone of all theories which regard man and his affairs . . . does it suit his nature in general: does it suit his nature as modified by his habits?"

What, then, shows us "the expedient" for man? "The mature judgment of the species."

"The individual is foolish. The multitude for the moment is foolish when they act without deliberation: but the species is wise—and when time is given it, as a species, it almost always acts right."

The organism regarded socially or individually has a certain restricted and relative infallibility. Thus it is that he is able to ridicule the folly of those "who draw up a bill of indictment against a whole nation."

"*I do not*," he says, "*vilify theory and speculation*—no—because that would be to vilify reason itself. But all theories with regard to man must alike be submitted to the touch-stone—does it suit his nature in general—his nature as modified

by his habits." The measure of truth and standard of right gained by the purely speculative
intellect, apart altogether from the experience of
the race, is as arbitrary as it is vague—mere
abstract notions of the private judgment may hit
on the truth here and there, but usually end in the
invention of an arbitrary truth of things " in
themselves "—and fantastic visions of a reality
never to be approached by the reason of man.

This is the scepticism which has been so freely
imputed to Newman—but, in fact, it is a scepticism which he was ever attacking and exposing.
Truth, thus conceived, he is continually reminding
us, is simply unattainable. It is truth as it lies in
things—as it lies in the world—truth as it is
arrived at by slow evolution in Society, in ideas,
in religions—truth as it is found in man—that we
are in search of.

*He does not deny the existence of eternal
truths*—ascertainable by individuals or established
in philosophical systems,—but when they are taken
as pure abstractions, when they are conceived
artificially and without reference to their
historical evolution in humanity—they are
barren: they seem " not sufficiently commanding to form a basis for public union and
action," they seem no longer to live. Truth,
therefore, for him—not only in theology,
but in philosophy, is not to be taken as something
abstract and detached but, as in a picture of
the Virgin Mother, in the very bosom of

Humanity—clinging to her and lost in her embrace.

In this manner then expediency and truth are to be conceived in order that we may reconcile the ideal and the real—: in order that the God of things as they ought to be may so become incarnate in things as they are, as to direct them to that permanent ideal reality which is ever approached but never gained—ever future but ever reigning over and guiding the present.

What, then, are the tests of the truth of ideas as they are found expressed and represented in an institution, a state, an organism?

Coherency or consistence is the statical, life the dynamic, test of truth.

The test of the truth of ideas is their capacity to live and the criterion of their having life is their power to grow, to reconcile, to assimilate, to go forth in many directions at once.

The test of dynamic truth is life. The test of life is growth. But there is also a logical test of dynamic truth—it must be shown to be one, to be proceeding from one source, to be, logically, a development. If something is advanced as true, because it has apparently grown from an acknowledged truth, and yet is obviously inconsistent with that truth—a false claim is made for it: it is a corruption. Such a later truth developed from an earlier may not be verbally developed: it may be developed by events rather than by conscious speculation,—but it must be possible to show that it does not contradict the forms in which it appeared at an earlier stage, so as to create a break in continuity.   For evolution has a logical side to it; a logic of events inherent in it; and development in ideas must be amenable to a logical test—the test of logical sequence.   It need not, of course, express itself in the form of the syllogism;—but it must be able to show that it has not, at any particular stage, lost logical continuity, for it is by a logical test, in the first place, that we find to what subject-matter an idea belongs.

Truth, then, in religion is rendered amenable to certain tests.

If religion is a necessary element in man and must not be simply destroyed or explained away, we must attempt to find what is the best religion for man.   And the manner in which we must find it is this: we must find what kind of truth we want and what kind of spokesman or expression of that truth.

There is an ethical and a religious process going on in the world as well as the cosmic, though all alike may owe their origin to the last and be ultimately resolvable into it. To the ethical process answers in man what is called the moral sense.   To the cosmic process answer the five senses, to the religious element in man— *a religious development in humanity.*

Man has developed this religious element in various ways—but he has, in a particular manner, become conscious of what is necessary as a basis of the religious idea.   It must represent as far as possible the sum of the religious ideas and the religious experiences of the race as a whole;—it must be one for all;—it must be Catholic. It must be living, that is—it must show itself able to assimilate or able to meet and account for, what is apparently opposed to it—:

It must continue, on a Catholic basis, the great experiment of man on his religious side. It must fulfil the function which it came into the world to carry out; it must have always the same general character in the opinion both of friends and foes. It must preserve its type and it must have within it the power to express itself.

In this way Newman's tests: preservation of type: continuity of principles: power of assimilation: early anticipation: logical sequence: and chronic continuance—will apply to that organism in which the religious idea and the developments of the religious element in man are attempted, as well as to the developments taken one by one.

If that organism, which humanity has developed within itself, perishes, it is scarcely possible to imagine how humanity is to attain its purpose. It is the great experiment of the human race to become religiously conscious of itself and to find what it is which it relies on in itself in matters of religion;—where the pivot is on which it turns;— where the sense of touch is which it uses—where the eyes are with which it sees—in matters of religion. Now the Catholic Church being the *one communion* in the world which makes the Catholic idea and universal unity *its basis* and *its ideal*, Newman inquires whether that Church may not be the organism required.

Prof. Fairbairn says that Newman ought to have set out first to find what was the germ idea of Christianity;—and he even goes so far as to tell us what it was.

But the problem Newman has set before himself was to find some scientific mode of discovering the type, for the simple reason that " what the germ is " is precisely the matter in dispute, *nor can we, in spiritual things, discover a germ except from the nature of its growth.*

Protestants having come to different conclusions, Newman suggests that their method may have been wrong and that his method may turn out more successful.

His object is to find out whether there are not a series of tests—brought from other kinds of development—which may be applied to the Catholic conception of what is the germ : because it may turn out that the Catholic conception, assumed by all Protestants to be so false as not to be worth investigating, is, on the whole truer than the others—while what is called the " *main idea of Christianity* " is in the process of expressing itself and cannot be known in its completeness till Christianity itself has run out its course. If the Catholic conception turns out to be truer and more in accordance with the most rigidly scientific series of tests we can apply, and the modification acknowledged on all hands does but show the power of assimilation found in all healthy organisms, may it not turn out that Christianity itself owes more to Catholicism and the world to Christianity than has hitherto been perceived?

The world itself may perhaps have discovered, through the Church, what is the real value of its religious element and where it can trust it.

It is clear that some germ there must have been in the religion called Christian which was able to produce what has followed from it. It is possible that the germ which grew was not the "main idea of Christianity" as it existed in the mind of its founder. It is possible;—but not very probable, and if the main idea was not the germ from which what is called Christianity grew, then the main idea of Christianity perished very early and something merely incidental grew up instead.

But something of this kind may *possibly* have happened to the religious idea itself from the very first. The act of the mind by which it makes human experience a different thing from the experience of the brutes: the conception of order: the ethical and religious idea in the individual— may not be the germ of the religious development of man as we see it. It may be, he ought to return to his earliest religious and mystical instincts, and reject all the developments as corrupting if he is to get a pure religion—the true religion of humanity. It may be he ought to appeal to a primitive church in which no developments at all have been made: of which Christianity,—in its purest form, is but a corruption.

But, in that case, he will find himself bound to make developments of his own as soon as ever he comes into contact with " action," and these may also be corruptions : and, if he doubts the religious process which has begun late in the history of the animal called man—may he not have equal reason to doubt the cosmic process by which he has become man at all?   And, in that case, he must set himself in opposition to the cosmic process in others as well as in himself for the cosmic process also goes forth (when viewed intellectually) on an intellectual assumption.

(3).—NEWMAN AS SCEPTIC AND EMPIRICIST.

(1)

"The problem," says Dr. Fairbairn, "as to
the evolution of the Church, the headship of the
supreme Pontiff, and his *ex Cathedra* infallibility,
is historical and soluble only by methods of historical research, which does not begin by *a priori*
definitions and determinations of one class of
growths as "corruptions" and another as
"developments," but simply observes the process,
the factors, and the results. Hence we must do
two things (a) find the germ, viz. :—the body or
system of truth, in its primitive or least developed
state, and (b) study the successive conditions under
which it lived, their action on it, its action on
them. The germ is simple, but the conditions are
complex and varied."

Dr. Fairbairn is telling Newman what he
ought to have done in order to realize the purpose
which he set before him in the " Essay on Development." In a note he enumerates Newman's tests
of the development of an idea—" the preservation
of the idea " itself; "continuity of principles,"
and so forth. "These," he says, "are so many
principles of prejudgment. So independent is

Newman of historical research that he does not condescend to any critical search after the idea that is to be preserved."

Newman might have ventured to remark on this astonishing piece of criticism that he conceived it was "the germ" as the body or system of truth in its undeveloped state which was the very question in dispute; it is "the idea"—a method of ascertaining which he is suggesting in his Essay, because there is so great a division of opinion as to what the idea is. To say that he is to begin by setting forth the germ "as a body of truth" and to say that the germ is simple, is to beg the question. The reason why Newman wrote his Essay was in general terms because mankind are hopelessly at variance as to what "the germ" and the idea are. He suggests that the reason why men are so much at variance about them is (1) because they have not hit upon the right method of finding them, (2) because, possibly, the idea is of so profound a description that it was expressed, at first, in terms which look like contradictions, (3) because the idea has not yet been fully expressed at all, but, from the very fact of its depth, has only given forth its extreme propositions, its antitheses, and that, from the very nature of the case, it is left to time, by reconciling these antitheses to give, one after another, all the aspects of the idea until the day shall arrive when we have got the sum of them, reconciled all the differences and attained the full expression of the idea. And (4) because the idea, even if it was at the birth of Christianity fully expressed (which if it was a deep one is impossible) was expressed in words with very few of which we are now acquainted. At the best we have a very short account even of the germ. When, therefore, he speaks, as he does, of "the preservation of the type," he is dealing with that obvious external expression of the idea which appears plainly in the face of history and with regard to which there is no difference of opinion. For instance; theories about the nature of "the kingdom" may be very numerous; the Christian conception of "the kingdom" may, at first, have been a crude one;— but there is no doubt that the Gospel is announced as the coming of the Kingdom of God. With such a fact it is possible to deal consistently with Newman's theory; but with the germ as a system of truth it is impossible to begin with dealing— for the nature of that system is the question in dispute and must come last, not first.

But Newman was not aiming at so much even as this. He was not aiming at finding the germ even at the end of his Essay. He was but suggesting a method which he thought might give a clue as to the manner in which the *nature* of "the germ" might be discovered. Now the Idea, as we have it, "in germ" (if we must use the expression), in the few words which are left to us in the documents of Christianity, does contain bold paradoxes, broad antitheses, apparent contradictions. From this fact as well as from the obscurity directly arising from the distance of time have arisen profound differences among Christians.

Sceptics have found great reason for triumph in these differences. Some of them have suggested that the reason is that in Christianity there was no idea at all; but only a series of incoherent propositions and that Christians were kept together, not by an idea the study of which always kept showing its depth and truth by reconciling opposites, accounting for contradictions, realizing itself on many sides at once,—but by personal loyalty to a character whose greatness could not well be exaggerated but whose depth and capacity in the region of ideas had come to be very much overestimated.

That Christianity had not at its basis some profound idea, not fully expressed but in the process of realization, seems improbable from the fact of the vigorous intellectual unity (amid the greatest mass of differences in history) of the Christian Church. But if this vigorous united intellectual life of the Church with its interior consistency and power to throw aside what it accounted heresy does not come into consideration at all, what proof is there that there was an idea? What proof is there that there was not an original, radical contradiction in the " germ " as there is now in the views taken of it? To what else can we have recourse? To a harmony of Gospel teachings? To somebody's theory of reconciliation? To some proof that Christ is God? To a proof of miraculous interference? But such proceedings all begin by assuming a notion so arbitrary and gratuitous that they seem hardly worth the labour

they must certainly entail.   If great toil has been
endured and great results have been attained by
persons professedly building on so narrow a
ground as the remote chance that an utterly
anarchical Christendom is founded on a great
interiorly consistent idea,—it is because men have
done so only professedly;—the profound unity
which is found in historical Christianity giving the
real basis of hope—often expressed with extraordinary simplicity—by persons who, in controversy, pretend to scout the very conception of
external unity.

Newman considers that the growth of the
Christian Church is a proof that there is an idea;
that the fact of its varied developments and its
power of assimilation and its capacity to flourish in
different soils and among various races shows that
the idea has great vitality and great depth.   There
is an idea; but the idea is not only deep, but so
deep,—so connatural to the heart of man,—that
in its first expression it partook of man's external
differences just because it was founded in his
interior unity.   There were not only apparent, but
real differences, in the Primitive Church, between
one Christian teacher and another; and it was only
after centuries, in some cases, that these differences
could be reconciled in a higher unity.   But, if
they were so reconciled at last, it was the persis-
tance, continuity and permanence of the Christian
type which rendered the reconciliation possible.
Such differences, then, between men who held the
idea in its inchoate form as expressed in the Chris-

tian type do but prove how deep the idea must be, which, after it had more fully developed, was able to reconcile them. In this manner Newman found that the theory of development, not only removes a difficulty, but becomes a positive argument for the depth and truth of the idea contained in Christianity. The idea was so profound and brought together natures so different that it came to be expressed, at first, in apparent, and, at the moment, in real contradiction; but it united these natures from below in a bond of instinctive unity the nature of which was not explained till centuries of struggle and polemic had passed away. Only when the great sayings of the Gospel and the teachings of Peter and Paul have been lived out and realized; only, when, through the working out, in every age, of all the aspects of the idea the sum of the aspects has been ascertained and all differences thereby reconciled, will the idea itself stand forth in its fullest expression.

In other words, Newman suggests the probability (our differences being caused as they are) that it is by the world's living out the Ideal that we shall get the true development of the Idea.

It is only when humanity has done, as a whole, what in his time and degree the individual is bidden to do, the will of the Ideal, that the doctrine of the Ideal shall be known by humanity.

When man shall have done the will and lived out the ideal, then only shall he know the doctrine and the idea.

To Newman the idea contained in the germ is

even more than this.   It is the Idea which, as he
conceives, not only lies at the root of man's being,
but is intrinsic to the nature of "the cosmic
process"—viewed as containing and accounting
for the ethical and the religious.   It is neither
religious nor irreligious; but the basis of all
religion, of all idea and of all being.   It is the
Idea at whose birth from the Divine mind—where
it had lived from all eternity—all the Sons of God
shouted for joy; it is the Idea in accordance with
which the Divine will formed, evolved and brought
into shape the world and drew man forth as from
the dust of the earth.   It is the Idea which, while
men slept, still, through the night, worked on.

Again : it is the treasure hid in a field, which
each man must seek for himself and which, as his
ideal, he shall find; but which, as the Idea,
humanity itself has ever sought and must ever seek,
and only at the last shall find.

It is the pearl of great price which—if a man
sell all that he has, he shall be able to gain; and
for which humanity must spend all that she is as
well as all that she has or ever she wholly possess
it.

It is the idea which gives forth in sanctity the
axioms of action on which is based the ideal; but
which, as Idea, can only then be realized when
these axioms of action have been translated into
terms of thought.

Newman, then, who does but hint at the
intrinsic nature of the Idea and rather leaves room
for the evolution of " the conscience " and " moral

sense " from what he calls a " combination " of natural causes than attempts to express a theory of the immanence of the Idea in the cosmic process, suggests in the Essay on Development a new method of ascertaining the centre of vitality in " the germ " from a consideration of the external history of the Idea. What is permanent; what still has life; what shows by the testimony of history and witnesses external to Christianity, a continuity in the Christian type—that is what witnesses to the centre of vitality in " the germ." It is the external history of the Idea in the world,— an Idea which is in the process of expression, that we find the best representation we can get of the true nature of " the germ."

As it had taken many ages to develope a few aspects of the Idea, before Christianity came into the world, so, according to Newman, it may take humanity many thousands of ages before it is able to discover, by the slow process of development, what " the germ " is " as a system of truth."

And yet it is " the germ—as a system of truth "—which Dr. Fairbairn tells us Newman ought to have begun by ascertaining; it is this idea (working from the foundation of the world, and, by hypothesis, only to be realized at the end of it) which Newman should neatly and succinctly set forth before attempting to deal with its development at all.

Dr. Fairbairn thus turns the method of Newman upside down and thinks that by so doing he has demonstrated its absurdity. He tells

H

Newman that he ought to have begun by ascertaining the intrinsic nature of the idea—which Newman is attempting to show it must take, and has taken, ages only partially to realize. Newman had no business to suggest that, if the idea was deep and because the idea had been shown to appeal to a vast variety of minds—it would, from the nature of the case, take time to reconcile and sum up all the aspects of it. He ought himself, it seems, to have performed the task of ages, reconciled all the aspects, accounted for all the differences, and resolved Christianity into its highest unity. It is because the Liberal theologians had seemed to him to be attempting (all unconsciously) this totally impossible task, that Newman suggests there may have been something fundamentally mistaken in their method.

(2)

How, then, does Newman come to speak of " *the preservation of an idea* " the internal nature of which he cannot describe?

Here Dr. Fairbairn has made a mistake, which, though apparently slight, illustrates his fundamental misconception of Newman's argument. Newman does not speak of the preservation of the idea. He speaks of the preservation of the type. The idea itself is too deep, too obscure and too large to be described. It is of its very nature that, in religion, the idea should be vague, inchoate, on its way to expression and not at any given time fully expressed. Were it not so religion would be a philosophy or a science from the starting point.   The relation of the thoughts, doctrines, and aspects of a religion to one another may indeed form a science and become a theology. And then the test of the truth of the science; the test of the value of the theology;—is the test which shows whether the synthesis thus attempted has been successful, and this test is the statical test of truth;—the test of consistency.   But the science of religion called theology is only concerned with the relation of doctrines to one another so far as they have been able to express themselves and develope in terms of a particular age and a particular mode of thought.   It is not through theology, but through history and the application of scientific thought that religion can be regarded dynamically and as a living growth.   The Essay on Development, therefore, is a criticism of theology and not, in the first place, a theological work.

Having shown why " the germ " and the idea are beyond the immediate scope of the method, which is to give the means of ascertaining, not " the germ " and the idea, in their intrinsic character; but their extrinsic nature sufficiently for the purpose in hand; Newman makes his first critical test—the preservation of the type; because as the germ changes in its growth, it is possible (and he proves it to be inevitable) it should change both its " *stuff and its fashion* " as our bodies change their substance once in so many years; while identity can only be proved by the preserva-

tion of a certain continuity of character, and this is
described by Newman as the continuity of type.
To ascertain the type and its continuity it is not
necessary to ascertain the idea, which can only be
judged by what the type ultimately becomes.   To
ascertain the type it is only necessary to hear the
world's account of it, and to ascertain its continuity
it is only necessary to discover whether the world's
account of it remains the same.   This we do in all
other cases where action is concerned.   But the
Christian type was concerned in the first place, as
Matthew Arnold says,—with action, with practice,
with conduct.   The world's account is prejudiced
in the case of Christianity, as we know, and so is
Christianity's account of itself.   But what we want
to ascertain is whether there was a real breach in
continuity in the type.   If the world's account ever
remains the same, it will not be a proof that the
world's account is true, or that it is not prejudiced;
but it will prove that the type remains the same,
that it excites the same prejudices, calls out the
same criticism, arouses the same peculiar form of
hostility.

The objection of Dr. Fairbairn is, however,
in the first place, an objection to the use of any
a priori method.   But it is not a very just mode
of attacking a book, which professes to have made
a discovery as to the method in which a certain
thing should be done, to begin by saying that the
author must not allow himself to use the only
method in which any such discovery has ever been
made.   And yet in telling Newman that he ought

not to have used the *a priori* method, Dr. Fairbairn is doing no less; for it has been proved over and over again in book after book upon the principle of induction, that no discovery has been made by the use of the inductive method alone, but by the use of an hypothesis—either already existing in the mind or especially thought out for the occasion—and then by the use of deductive and inductive processes—until the first hypothesis is either proved or discarded. It is experiment applied to a clearly expressed hypothesis and hypothesis applied to long series of experiments— which bring about the discovery of new facts and new data in science; and not the use of experiment alone or the process of induction alone.

Moreover, it is not just to a book like the *Essay on Development* to attack its *a priori* method straight away as if Newman had used that method from a mere bias of his mind and theological tendency to argue in that manner. Newman has elaborately defended his use of this method; and to take no notice of the reasons which he gives in this particular case, for doing what has really been done in every case of the sort that occurs (whether the writers or discoverers have been conscious of it or not) is not really to criticize the book or the argument, but only to create prejudice and make room for that disparagement of the author's abilities which French and German writers have told us is the English substitute for literary criticism.

Now Newman's frank use of a hypothesis is

more scientific than the method of Liberal
Theologians, who make a hypothesis also, but
imagine that they are employed in merely getting
at the facts.

It is not my purpose to go through and restate
the whole argument of the Essay; but to remove
the prejudices against it and attempt to show
the manner in which they have arisen. Newman
makes a double hypothesis—the hypothesis of
Development as against those conservative theologians, who say that Roman doctrine is but
Primitive Christianity expressed in modern words;
and the hypothesis of an instinct of self-preservation in the Catholic organism which has taught it
what was food for it and what poison in the
religious nutriment with which it found itself
provided,—as against Protestants who hold that
the true idea of Christianity was corrupted from
the first.

It is the *gravamen* of Dr. Fairbairn's argument
against Newman that Newman arbitrarily intro-
duces " mechanical supernaturalism " in the infallibility of the Church, in order to get rid of what
he calls the element of " chance and coincidence "
to which Liberal theologians and sceptical writers
attribute the rise and growth of the Catholic
Church. I have already dealt with this charge on
the surface; now I must go through it in detail.

The charge is the original charge of philosophical scepticism (in a slightly different form)—
the charge brought against both Newman and
Pascal.

With regard to the interior argument used by
Pascal and Newman for the existence of the idea of
which they hold the Catholic Church to be the
latest and the highest expression, I shall deal hereafter.   In this place I shall deal with the charge
that Newman's conception of a " mechanical supernaturalism " excludes the Idea altogether; virtually
denies that the Idea is the cause of man's religious
development and substitutes an arbitrary supernatural conscience and ecclesiastical authority for
any use of the reason.

It is the charge that Newman substitutes a
Traditionalism, founded on a Hume's scepticism
and distrust of the reason, for a rational
metaphysic.

I must deal, then, first with Newman's treatment of the reason.

(3)

I have already admitted that Newman in his
" University Sermons " uses the presupposition of
Hume.   Dr. Fairbairn considers that he remained
philosophically a sceptic in Hume's sense to the
end; and that it was to supplement the impotence
of " an instrumental reason " " forsaken by God "
that Newman introduced first an arbitarily conceived " conscience " as a moral dictator and then
an infallible Church as the representative and guide
of the conscience.

Dr. Fairbairn, in illustration of the charge,
makes some of the quotations to which I have
already alluded.   As soon as Dr. Fairbairn made

his charge, however, Newman replied to it and Dr. Fairbairn answered that the reply does but substantiate the charge.

Newman had argued that, even on the presupposition of Hume, we are compelled to take the world offered us by the senses as an organic whole and to deal with it as such. Even if we allow that " custom " it is that has enabled us to do so, we have grounds of a similar nature for treating religion as an objective organic whole, though this " objective organic whole " has arisen, to all seeming, merely from a series of " impressions " on men's minds, and therefore remains subjective.

Dr. Fairbairn considers that Newman, in so arguing, leaves the scepticism of Hume where it was and merely builds upon it a religious world in the same way that Hume built upon it a world which was still really subjective, and our manner of dealing with which was supplied by custom and association. Dr. Fairbairn contends that Newman does but place authority in religion in the same position as Hume places custom; that the reason, with Newman, is a series of antecedents and consequents in the same way that, with Hume, it is a series of impressions and ideas; that the reason is left impotent and instrumental and the authority derived from " the moral sense cut off and divided from the reason is arbitrary, non-rational and mechanical. " My contention is," says Dr. Fairbairn, " that to conceive the reason as Dr. Newman does is to deny to it the knowledge of God and so to save faith by the help of a deeper unbelief."

Now it has been my contention that Newman absorbs, so as to transcend, Hume's doctrine. In his sermon on " Bigotry," etc., he shows that in order to act in accordance with the reason, considered, at first, as an instrument, we must and always do reason " with the whole man "; and, though we still use the reasoning faculty as an instrument, we use it as a living instrument organically connected with our whole being—connected organically with our conscience as truly as with our memory; though in the individual, in the concrete, there is no necessarily realised connection between the intellect and the affections—or the intellect and the conscience.   But an organic whole, when seen as organic by the mind, becomes object for the mind.   Hence Newman's objective religion.

When Newman says that there is no " necessary connection " between the conscience and the reason, he is speaking popularly.   He does not mean to deny that the organic connection remains, but he means that the organic connection sometimes ceases to be realized.   He uses the expression, because he wishes to admit that the organic connection between the conscience and reason is not " necessary " in the same degree as the organic connection between (*e.g.*) the reason and the memory—a fact which is demonstrable, for the reason could not survive the total loss of memory but the reason sometimes survives the

apparent loss of the moral sense; and appears, for
a time, to be even stronger when the affections are
diminishing in power. Newman lays himself
open to the charge of scepticism by making these
admissions in its favour, because he does not wish
it to be possible for anyone to say that he has left
an element in it unconsidered or treated it, in any
case, unfairly. Dr. Fairbairn considers that
Newman leaves the reason vacant and idle " till it
has received the deliverances of the conscience ";
but Newman never says that the reason is idle: on
the contrary, he says that it is " restless," ever
seeking a system or a unity; but he contends that
on this very ground, it is continually finding a
system which it conceives to be absolute; it is ever
finding a unity which is not the absolute unity—
(in the individual and in the concrete) when the
religious sense does not exist,—because it rightly
conceives that it is bound to acquiesce in a system
until it is proved that the system is incomplete.
The evil is not in the reason of man taken in the
mass, which would go on to make a synthesis of all
history and would find in history the witness to
religion; for the very restlessness of the reason
makes it dissatisfied with one system after another,
because it becomes aware, when experience is
given it, that its synthesis is not complete. The
evil is not in the reason, abstractly considered, for
the reason, abstractly considered, is not subject to
time. But the evil is in the reason, in the
individual, in the concrete,—where men have
learnt to regard the moral sense, the religious sense

and the affections as obstacles—and nothing but causes of bias, to the use of the reason.   This is the isolation of the reason which Newman deplores —precisely as Burke deplores it in those who attempt to free the reason from what they call the artificial civilization of history, and talk about the " noble savage " as the highest type of humanity.

Newman then, can turn round upon Hume and say " You are doing in metaphysic just what Rousseau did in history."   In a similar manner, Newman shows the organic connection of the conscience with the reason ; shows that the conscience, in its development, needs the reason as well as the reason the conscience ; carries on this organic conception into history ; shows that the development of the religious idea in national religion and in the Catholic Church is analogous to the development of the conscience ; shows the *organic connection* of this development of the religious idea in the Catholic Church with the development of the reason and " the progress of the scientific temper " ; and then sets forth the hypothesis of an instinct of self-preservation in the religious organism (infallible in the detection of food and poison) as completing the parallel of religious development in the knowledge of religious subjects with scientific development in the knowledge of scientific subjects.   That is, Newman suggests that, as science can assume a certain relative infallibility with regard to its main teaching, because it has its subject matter before it, and can apply its tests with certainty ; so religion can assume a certain relative infallibilty with regard to the subject matter of religion which is constantly before it in the experiences of the race, and can apply, to what has now become on its own grounds (in consequence of the differentiation of function inevitable to man) a distinct organism, *a definite series of tests;* not with such immediate certainty as science, for the subject matter in religion is still far more vague than in science, but with sufficient certainty for the purpose of carrying on the great religious and spiritual process .

(4)

Now let us turn to Dr. Fairbairn's attack and the quotations from Newman which he thinks bear out and justify his attack.   " The doctrine of the reason Cardinal Newman has stated is," says Dr. Fairbairn, " in the philosophical sense, essentially a sceptical doctrine."   And here is what Dr. Fairbairn regards as Newman's earliest statement (with his later notes appended): " There is no necessary connection," says Newman, " between the intellectual and moral principles of our nature —that is," he adds, " as found in individuals, in the concrete," " and we can arrive at truth but accidentally, if we merely investigate by what is commonly called reason, which is in such matters but the instrument at best, in the hands of the legitimate judge, spiritual discernment."

" Because," Newman adds in his notes, " we may be reasoning from wrong principles, principles unsuitable to the subject matter reasoned upon.

Thus, the moral sense or 'spiritual discernment' must supply us with the assumptions to be used as premises in religious inquiry."

"And here," says Dr. Fairbairn, "is his latest statement."

"In its versatility, its illimitable range, its power of concentrating many ideas on one point, it (the reason) is for the acquisition of knowledge all important or rather necessary; with this drawback, however, in its ordinary use, that in every exercise of it, it depends for its success upon the assumption of prior acts similar to that which it has itself involved, and therefore is reliable only conditionally. Its process is a passing from an antecedent to a consequent, and according as the start so is the issue. In the province of religion if it be under the happy guidance of the moral sense, and with teachings which are not only assumptions in form, but certainties, it will arrive at indisputable truth, and then the house is at peace; but if it be in the hands of enemies, who are under the delusion that its arbitrary assumptions are self-evident axioms, the reasoning will start from false premises, and the mind will be in a state of melancholy disorder. But in no case need the reasoning faculty itself be to blame or responsible, except if viewed as identical with the assumptions of which it is the instrument; as such I have viewed it, and no one but Dr. Fairbairn would say as he does—that the bad employment of a faculty was a division or a contradiction and 'a radical antagonism of nature' and 'the death of the natural proof' of a God."

If, then, the reason is not to blame when we reason to a false conclusion, it is entirely separable from the conscience; and it is not only a mere instrument but an instrument unconnected " with the whole man." What hope is there, then, for the individual, if he has started on false principles that he will ever get right again? His very loyalty to his reason will but lead him further and further astray.

But Newman means exactly the opposite to what Dr. Fairbairn supposes him to mean. He means that the reason is an instrument, indeed, but an instrument organically connected with the whole man. If it is not realized by the reason that it is thus connected with the whole man, the reason will become more and more disconnected with the other elements in man, and the man will cease to be at unity with himself. The reason, however, may not be to blame—for it may be the memory only which is to blame. Surely Dr. Fairbairn will admit this: that if a process of reasoning is complete but issues in a false conclusion because, at the start, an important fact was forgotten, it is not the reason which is to blame but the memory. The organic connection with the memory remains and is even proved by the fact that the reason goes wrong because the memory is mistaken. To show that this is the case; to show that the reason may complete its process on perfectly logical grounds, and yet be wrong if the memory is at fault is not to show that the memory and the reason are fatally divided one from the other, but to show that they are organically connected.

Dr. Fairbairn observes that Newman by making the reason " a process of antecedents and consequents," falls into the notion of an infinite series. But Newman does not imply anything of the kind. He says that the process of the reason is a process of antecedent and consequent and that consequently, if the reason is isolated from the memory or the moral sense, the whole mind ceases to be at unity with itself, falls into a state of melancholy disorder and will tend to go round for ever in that circle of errors which is infinite. Newman, that is, holds that the series began, and begins necessarily, in the reason's use of facts ; but if the reason gets disconnected with the facts or has not a sufficient acquaintance with the facts, it is left to devour itself in an impotent ideology.

He does not mean that the reason is without the potentiality of finding unity from within itself ; of finding its own unity. It is, on the contrary, because it must assume its own unity that it can be contemplated as a separate faculty at all. The fact that the potentiality is there is the fact on which Newman is insisting when he appears to Dr. Fairbairn to be making a division of the faculties. But the potentiality is not only a potentiality to assume its own unity ; it is by the use of this power that knowledge becomes possible at all. This is why Newman says that reason is

all important or rather necessary to the acquirement of knowledge. As soon as reason begins to
act it begins to reconcile " the whole man " in a
unity, whose possibility it is bound, from its own
nature consciously or unconsciously to assume from
the first. This assumption is given in the reason
itself, or else its process of " antecedents " and
" consequent " would itself be irrational. Newman,
however, is not dealing with what speculation
shows us is given in the reason; but with reason in
the concrete; and, in the concrete even reason's
assumption of its unity is a thing very seldom fully
realized by the reason; and not until it has been
educated from without does it become aware either
of its special powers or of its limitations.

It is on its limitations that Newman is insisting
—because its limitations, in the concrete and in the
individual, are what philosophers seemed to him
chiefly to ignore. That it has a unity in itself;
that it is ever seeking unity from its very nature;
that it assumes the possibility of unity from the
start—Newman takes as assumed as its characteristic—in the fact that it both " has an illimitable
range " and gives us " the power of concentrating
many ideas on one point." What he thinks is
forgotten or is not realized is that its true use
must result in something more than a reconcilation
with itself. It must start, if it is to succeed, with
the assumption that it has to reconcile the whole
man; it must start on the assumption that it lies
already in a higher unity of which its own unity is
but a reflexion—the unity of the conscience and the

moral sense and all the faculties of man.   The
fact that the reason and the conscience belong to
this higher unity is assumed by religion and it is
the value of religion that it insists on the fact of
this unity—as the basis—before the unity has been
philosophically realized; before the individual has
been able for himself to resolve the conscience and
the reason, on philosophical grounds, into a higher
unity.   The reason, Dr. Fairbairn thinks, according to Newman, " is emptied of those constitutive
and constructive qualities which make it a reason."
But this is because he imagines Newman to conceive of the reason as a dead, external instrument;
whereas Newman conceives of the reason as a
living instrument organically connected with the
moral sense and the memory and the other
faculties.

And, consequently, the abuse of the reason,
according to Newman, consists—not in its being
considered as connected vitally with the other
faculties nor in its being considered as an instrument—; but in its being disconnected with the
other faculties in such a manner as to make it
indifferent to the conscience and the other
faculties.   Great as it is and necessary not only to
all knowledge but also to the conscience and the
moral sense, it is not great enough to assume itself
as superior to the conscience; to assume itself as
the sole originating cause of man's conception of
religion and morality.   The conscience could not
have come to be what it is without the reason; but
the conscience is not a mere result of the reason

I

owing its place to a hereditary reverence. It has
been developed by the reason, as dogma has been
developed by the reason, but as it does not owe its
development to the reason only, so it does not
owe its origin to the reason only.   Its origin is
in the unknown or Divine or dependent on some
special growth of the affections.   The affections
could not have taken such a form without the use
of the reason nor can the Divine origin of
conscience exclude the fact of its evolution   in
accordance with laws of reason or its creation (if
it was created) by the exercise of that reason which
is called Divine.   It is as organically connected
with the reason as the reason is connected with it.
But, as the representative of the affections or of
the Divine reason, it expresses a conclusion which
reason in the individual and in the concrete comes
to and works towards through a laborious process.
It is the value of the conscience and of religion to
give to the reason an assurance that there is a
truth at the end of the journey which   makes
worth while the process; a truth without which,
indeed, conscience and religion tell us,   reason
could not even exist, but a truth which the reason
has to realize, through a painful process, in terms
of its own.   This truth is the absolute unity of
the Universe.   But the reason of the individual is
confronted with the whole process of discovering
this unity in what appears at first an infinity of
difference.   The individual cannot hope by
himself completely to realize this unity.   It is
only reason in the mass which will be able to reach,

at the last, the conclusion with which conscience begins, and in the hope of which reason (even when most sceptical) is always consciously or unconsciously working.

" The only justification," says Dr. Fairbairn, " of Cardinal Newman's doctrine would have been the reduction of conscience and reason to a higher unity."   But it is the fact that they must be regarded as lying in a higher unity that Newman is insisting on; while the fact that they can only be resolved philosophically into this unity, after long ages, is the basis of his method:—To this reduction of conscience and reason to a higher unity, Newman would say that he had attempted to contribute his quota, by showing that it is by reason *in the mass*, working in the light of the hope which conscience and religion give, that this reduction of conscience to a higher unity will, at last, be made by humanity. But to say that Cardinal Newman ought to have done it himself would seem to Newman like telling him that he ought to be the human race. It was on this ground that Newman hesitated to accept philosophical systems which seemed to assume that a resolution of all the opposed terms in the controversy into their ultimate unity might be possible before the human race had lived out the idea or " the System of God " in accordance with which it had been created or evolved.

The reason in the individual, then, according to Newman is defective or limited in the following respects :—

(1) Because it does not necessarily realize its organic connection with the moral sense or the affections, regarding them, not as making its process richer and truer, but as causes of bias only.

(2) Because it does not necessarily realize its connection with reason in the mass or in the race or with the past.

(3) Because, although it is always attempting to gain an absolute unity, it does not necessarily realize all the elements which it has got to resolve into in that unity in order that the unity should be absolute; has nothing but education from without—, from the reason in the mass, to make it realize that the very brain which is its material instrument or expression is as much a development from the past as the language which it is compelled to use in order to act at all; and that, consequently, it fails to realize its true position in the individual and in the race; that, thus regarded, it is neither a first " reason " in humanity starting free from the hereditary developments of past ages —as Rousseau unconsciously assumed—or a last " reason " in humanity, able to act independently of the future, as if it could resolve into their ultimate unity all the elements in humanity (or at least the most important) as Dr. Fairbairn and many other philosophers with a system unconsciously assume.

This, Newman thinks, suggests the place of religion in the development of man.   Because the individual cannot start fair or sum up the past so as to express the whole idea on which humanity is living or resolve all thought into its ultimate unity—or bring about a kind of philosophical day of judgment and make his system the final judge of quick and dead,—therefore religion comes forward to give man hope; telling him that he may in the long run succeed in his philosophic endeavour, but that, as an individual, he must begin on the assumption that what he wishes to realize is in the process of being realized; that he is not the first man in humanity or the last and that therefore all he can do in philosophy is to contribute his quota, as one in the midst of many, to the process of which he must thus assume himself to be a part, or submit to philosophic or religious annihiliation.

The reason why philosophers of such extraordinary greatness have fallen into the still more extraordinary error of regarding the human race as coming to the end of its developments in their own time—so as to lie before them as a whole—has, surely, been that they have either failed to give religion any commanding position at all or have acknowledged its influence as a thing of the past and ignored its necessity to the present and the future. I am far from saying that Dr. Fairbairn or Hegel (who has been accused of this error) altogether fall into it, but in insisting that no philosophic conception of reason and conscience (the chief subject matter of the world's whole development) can be worth much which does not resolve them, at once, in philosophic terms into a higher unity—all such reasoners are falling into that finality which they condemn (and falsely condemn) in the Catholic Church.

It was the good fortune of Christianity to fall into this error as soon as it came into the world and expect the day of judgment or ever that generation had passed away. By committing the error in a manner which time could at once and finally disprove—the error itself, though constantly recurring in a slighter form, has preserved the Church from the possibility of ever succumbing to it altogether and has compelled the individual to realize that the most dogmatic assertion of the Church, though final for him in his ordinary conduct, can but be provisional for the race and conditional in its very nature; so that Pere Simon, while submitting to the great mass of the human reason in religion as represented by authority, could still believe that in the long run both he and the authority which condemned him would prove to be right—he, in the main thesis which he had advanced, and the authority, in condemning the manner in which he advanced it as not sufficiently proved to convince, or too crude to take its place in the slowly advancing system of the Church or, again, too complete, too self-sufficing to find a place in the midst of ideas which, if larger, were still inchoate, still going on to completion.

" The only justification of Cardinal Newman's doctrine would have been the reduction of conscience and reason to a higher unity; his last condemnation," continues Dr. Fairbairn, " is his distinction and division of the faculties, for it involves our nature in a dualism which makes real knowledge of religious truth impossible. There is unity neither in the man who knows nor in the truth as known."

Newman, on the contrary, holds that the truth can only be known to " *the whole man* "; that it cannot be known to the reason alone or to the memory alone or to the moral sense alone; and the proof of it is that only when every faculty is given its place—is man found to be, as a matter of experience, at unity with himself; only when the reason has recognized the affections and the moral sense as no mere causes of bias, but as making the reason richer—and the moral sense and the affections have come to realize that the reason is essential to the acquirement of knowledge, even in their own domain, is " the house at peace."

" Make a present," says Dr. Fairbairn, " of true premises to a faculty merely ratiocinative and they will be to it only as algebraic symbols, not as truths of religion; its deduction may be correct but it will have no religious character."

Does Dr. Fairbairn, then, deny that we have any faculty which is merely ratiocinative? Would he deny that when the memory receives a religious truth it merely remembers it? This is to deny distinctions so completely as to make a mere jumble of the faculties; but Newman neither makes an absolute division, nor merely confuses one faculty with another. He regards the faculties as *distinct* (as the memory from the ratiocinative faculty);—but though he regards the faculties as distinct enough to be named as mankind have invariably named them, he regards them as organically connected. And this is not to make a jumble of the faculties, nor is it to divide in such a manner as to isolate, one from the other.

Newman is considered to have fallen into the very abyss of individualistic nominalism because, writing in the "Grammar of Assent," he does justice even to individualistic nominalism; shows that it is a necessary stage of the mind's process; and that there is no royal road to truth which does not pass through it; but he shows also that, in religion, there is only one way of absorbing and transcending it, because even individualistic nominalism is compelled, if it will have religious truth at all (and it cannot afford to obliterate religion from the subjects it must treat) to regard it, not as something abstract and detached, but as "lying in the bosom of humanity" and "lost in her embrace." That is, in religion as in everything else, the individualist, having become aware of his own subjectivity and that his mind is the only criterion of truth he has, goes on to see that, in so regarding his mind, he has discovered its objectivity; and from the objectivity he goes on to perceive that he is object among other objects— related to them by this very objectivity; that this relation involves others and that, not until he has realized, as far as he may, all these relations, can he come back to himself and use the objective criterion he has found, which is, for him, still his only ultimate criterion, with an objective validity. Everything in the world is, as the individualist shows, subjective to the mind; and religion like everything else; but everything that can be viewed as organic by that very process becomes object, and religion, if it can be shown to be organic, becomes likewise object for the mind. Mind, in other words, must first have gained through the consciousness of its subjective individuality a knowledge of that organic unity which makes it object for itself, before it can recognize, on grounds of reason, the objective character of science from its being organic (though science is still organically incomplete) or the objective character of religion from its being organic (though religion is still organically incomplete).

But it is more important for man that he should recognize the objective nature of religion from its being an organic whole (though still going onwards as a living organism) than that he should recognize the objective nature even of the sciences, for with religion he must deal at once; from religion he usually gets the first external intimation that all his faculties have to be used together, and that his moral sense and his religious sense and his affections must be at once associated with his reason and his reason with them. For religion alone claims to give to man the hope on which all the processes of his understanding must be founded if they are ever to realize the unity for which they cannot help even mechanically seeking;—namely, the hope, based on the assurance that an absolute unity is realizable because in an absolute unity all things are founded. Of this absolute unity, which is God, the authority which Newman puts in the place of Hume's custom, is the representative, because it is representative not only of man's reason, but of man's whole nature, so far as it has yet been found possible to give that nature any expression—at once social and coherent.

(5)

When reason has arrived at the necessity for an absolute, it does not necessarily find that absolute; and even it it find an absolute in religion it has not yet got beyond "absolute thing" and may still refuse to believe in "absolute Person."

And this is the point where Dr. Fairbairn more completely misunderstands Newman than anywhere else. Newman considers that the reason may arrive at a God as the expression of its own ultimate unity and so arrive at Pantheism, but he denies that the reason alone can arrive at that absolute unity which absorbs and expresses the whole man in Personality except the reason has learned "to make for the truth with the whole man." Reason can never make for the truth with the whole man except when it has learnt that there are no elements in man's nature which are to be set on one side as mere causes of bias; until it has learnt that the affections are as necessary to truth as the process of reason and that nothing is true, even to it, which is not able to pass uncontradicted through all the depths of man's being. Morality and religion aid in the realization of the object by bringing men into contact with the nature of things through action; and, though these cannot act without the reason, yet it is they, with the reason, which are creative and not reason alone; because it is they that give to reason that sense of reality which can only be felt by man when he becomes aware that all his faculties, exercised in their several ways with full energy,—the reason not stunted by the affections, the religious sense not eliminated by the reason,—are satisfied together and can acquiesce in a conclusion arrived at by man as an organic whole.

But how is man to find the nature of that, in which his whole being can rest satisfied? Only by refusing to exterminate all desires and fears as irrational which cannot be justified or accounted for at once by the use of the reason. Of these desires and fears, those which are implied " in the sense of sin " have usually been the very first which the reason, in its restless desire for a unity satisfactory to itself alone, has peremptorily exterminated as irrational. Dr. Fairbairn might say, though he does not say it, that the reason would here be acting inconsistently and that Newman in criticizing such action as the natural and almost inevitable course of the reason is only calling the reason itself irrational. But in criticizing the reason as exercised in time, in the individual and in the concrete, it is not saying anything more than that an energetic capacity for reasoning, from its very perfection, may become impatient of what, at first sight, must appear simply and obstinately opposed to it; and that it is necessary for the reason's perfection that it should deny the validity and the use of that for which it cannot give a reason. It is even right, as we learn from the history of philosophic thought, that reason should proceed from denying to affirming—for only through denial does the whole nature of what is denied become forced into expression. But, then, the reason in the individual cannot do this without the danger of a loss to the whole being at least for a prolonged period. It is the whole problem of sin. "Yea, hath God said?" "Does the conscience forbid?" "Well, even if God hath said, even if the conscience does forbid, it is only by trial that the truth can be found—let us try."

And what reason says is true, as far as it goes; it is only reasoned experience which shows that if everything is to be tried man will never be able to get at any straight line of life and plan of living; any course that can be pursued and achieved at all; for it is not reason, but experience, which shows that the choice of things which might be tried, is infinite.

The reasoned experience, then, in the race comes to the help of reason in the individual and says:—"These vague intimations which you distrust point to a fact. They are the hereditary instinct which warns us against what makes for the destruction of man. They are not really destructive of the reason, but though they seem to ignore

reasoning they are necessary to the preservation of the reason—nay, so necessary, so welded together are they with the course of nature and the cosmic process and so strict a line of orientation have they observed from the very first, that, vague as they are, the human race could not have remained in being had they not existed and been diligently attended to;—so that men have everywhere come to regard them with the greatest reverence, listen for what they may seem to say with the keenest attention and, even though they seem to contradict themselves on particular points, have everywhere come to regard them as oracles, as Divine intimations, as the voice of God in the soul of man."

Here reason in the mass, having come to regard man as an organic whole, not by the mere exercise of its special faculty, but by the force of circumstances combined with that exercise, comes to the aid, or to the correction, of reason in the individual. And this is the authority without, which answers to conscience within. Now Dr. Fairbairn is very angry with Newman because he finds the characteristic element in the conscience, in religion and Christianity, to be the fear of retribution. And he scoffs at Newman for quoting Lucretius as the best authority for describing Pagan religion. Dr. Fairbairn accuses Newman of finding the very idea of religion in the sense of sin. Newman does not say " the idea "—but the characteristic which distinguished religion externally, the typical element upon which an enemy of religion would fix. Newman quotes Lucretius as an external testimony to what a man going by reason alone finds offensive and unreasonable in religion. He hits at once upon its fear, its cowering terror, its sense of retribution. Dr. Fairbairn says that this fear was irrational; that Lucretius did right in condemning it, that it belonged to a religion which was by no means pure and which was almost entirely non-moral.

Ah,—but this is the very point! It is in this sense of retribution that the religious element showed its connection with morality; it is here that the thing especially characteristic of the religious conception of morals as opposed to the merely rationalistic conception of morals, began to grow up. It is at this point that religion comes first to be seen as an interpreter and an enforcer of the moral sense—beyond what the reason by itself would ever have discovered. True it is that superstition which regards the awful sanctity of the gods with a cowering dread is, at first, more like a Devil worship than the worship of God. But alas! such is the infinite pathos of human nature that it cannot make a step forward in the way of truth without at the same time falling into some error; and when man first began to feel for a Personal God—the God whose very Being is an awful sanctity—it was the sense of the contrast which first burnt itself into his heart; and the terror which results from his being so unlike that better self which he began vaguely to see in the Divine.

Reason, also, comes into the Divine presence; —and it comes, as the philosophers came, with a serene countenance,—easily and happily appreciating the infinite superiority of the Gods; and even if it appreciates their infinite nearness too, still it remains, even in the noblest,—" too much at ease in Zion." Philosophers could feel the Divine; they could draw nearer to God; but it was the simple and ignorant man, filled with superstition, who knew best his own unworthiness and who first detected the shadow of the cross even in the bright religions of Paganism; who best discerned that one awful sanctity in the Divine which was the first intimation to the religious sense of the one God whose character is holiness.

Reason, indeed, may give the Divine, with a rational morality, and gives it, as to the great philosophers of antiquity, so also to Göethe, to Matthew Arnold, to all the serener tempered and more classical of the poets; but it is the primitive religious sense—intimately connected with the intrinsic necessity of morality—which expects in the Divine the awful sanctity of one supreme and personal Being.

So we have with the ancients a high morality and a serene and reasonable sense of the Divine; but with Christianity the cross and sanctity—the very genius of morality;—and it is no longer the wisdom which knew not God,—which shall judge the world,—but the saints and the awful sanctity of God.

Philosophers, then, regarded superstition as

mere waste and disease; Newman regards it as man's way of getting a new development in a sanctity based on the Personality of God.

It is not a little strange that Dr. Fairbairn should pay so little heed to this characteristic element in Christianity which even Matthew Arnold gives as the reason of its prolonged success and its great value to conduct;—the seriousness it gave to life, which he considers the characteristic difference of Christianity from the prevailing temper of Paganism. But it is stranger still that he makes nothing at all of the originality of *sanctity* which the author of " Ecce Homo " regards as *the very creation of that high development of the religious sense which we call Christianity*.

(6)

Now the claim which a Catholic makes for his Church is not what Dr. Fairbairn supposes it to be. It is not that the Church is the Christian religion—(as Dr. Fairbairn supposes) for there is still much in the Christian religion which the Church has not expressed; it is that the Church alone keeps to the front, in however crude or immature a fashion, the typical teachings of Christianity, attempts to realize them without explaining them away, and in realizing them slowly brings out the Idea which gave them birth. Thus, with the Church, the Eucharist may be expresed in philosophical terms which to modern philosophy may appear crude, but these terms were intended to preserve the reality of the Presence which the Eucharist brings to man. So, again, the Church in describing the union of Christ with God insists on the reality and completeness of this union; and, whereas there are those outside the Church who say that it is a merely spiritual union, it is the habit of the Church to observe that this union is so intensely real and complete because it is spiritual. So with the Papacy and the kingdom of God on earth, however crude an expression the Papacy may be of the fact that the Church is a kingdom, it is the only way in which it was possible for the Church to insist on the reality of the kingship of Christ. It may acquire a deeper meaning and a further expression in the course of ages; but no clearer or more practical mode could have been conceived of keeping its reality before the minds of men.

So with the sense of sin, the doctrine of original sin and the teaching of St. Augustine may be insufficient for the time we live in;—but it represents a fact which has had its own special mode of development and on the reality of the fact the Church has ever insisted in a manner which cannot be mistaken.

A Catholic, then, claims for the Church that she has preserved as no other religious institution has done, the sense of reality in the great dogmas which represent Christianity; she has not allowed them to be explained away. The kingdom of Christ has not, with her, become a matter so vague that the word " kingdom " may mean little

J

more in the Christian Church than it means in
such an expression as "the animal kingdom."
The sense of sin has not been allowed to become
so vague as to make the notion of sanctity impossible. The Eucharist, while continuing to be a
memorial, has never become a mere memorial.
The Divinity of Christ has never become a mere
mode of expressing what is more than usually
heroic or virtuous.

In consequence of the preservation of the great
elements in Christianity as *real*, though sometimes
crudely and as it were pictorially expressed, the
special characteristics of Christianity still belong to
the Church; the main lines of its truths are preserved; the main conception of its sanctity remains.
The Catholic claims for the Church, then, that it
has preserved a dogma which is true and a conception of life which insists on sanctity—and that
these two things work together to produce both
truth and holiness. But the Catholic does not, therefore, consider, as Dr. Fairbairn thinks, that the
Church is his religion. In everything short of this
dogma and this sanctity the Catholic is ready to
admit that the Church has failed, again and again,
to realize its ideal or to be a complete representative of its religion.

(7)

A very considerable portion, then, of Dr.
Fairbairn's general indictment against the actual
dominion of the Church, a Catholic may readily
admit. Indeed, in some cases, he may go further

in reprobation of the line taken by authority than Dr. Fairbairn himself; for a large part of what Dr. Fairbairn has to say is directed against the Church only as an ecclesiastical institution.

In this sense it is certainly true that in maintaining the real nature of the kingdom of Christ, power has constantly been exercised in too absolute a manner, and the inevitable conservatism of all ancient instituions has been expressed in terms of an obscurantist nihilism. The Church, says Dr. Fairbairn, had in her hands the whole intellect of Europe before the Reformation; she is, therefore, responsible for the loss of the Reformers. The Church had in her hands the whole intellect of France before Voltaire and Diderot. "During centuries the Church had been supreme; hers had been the hands that made the men, hers the mind that made Europe; and if the issue of all her doings and endeavours were the revolt, could she be guiltless, or as wise as she must be to make her infallibility of any avail, or make it anything more than an ability to do great things if she only knew how?" Who pretends that the Church was guiltless? Indeed, there are few who would now deny that had the authorities treated the great pioneer of criticism, Simon, with common justice and common consideration, the chief weapons of 18th century scepticism would have been struck out of the hands of its most brilliant representatives and the Revolution in France, though it might still have been a revolt against feudalism might not have been, in any considerable degree, a revolt against Christianity or Catholicism; for Simon had seen how the freest criticism could be united with the most ardent belief in the truth of the Catholic religion and was consistent with a living Catholic religion alone, but, when he was condemned, every one of the points which he had made were turned against the Church which condemned him.

But if the minds of great ecclesiastics, like Bossuet, were unequal to the task of reconciling one side of the Church's development with another —is that a proof that the doctrines of the Church were responsible for the loss of Voltaire and Diderot? If the Church had in her hands the truth she could not have lost some of her greatest sons, it is argued. But if the Church had not the truth, who is responsible for the loss of the Church herself to the true teaching of Christ? If the Church is responsible for the loss of Voltaire, who is responsible for the loss of the Church? The failure of the Church to retain the true teaching of Christ was owing, Dr. Fairbairn thinks, to the fact that the germ was mistated and misrepresented by mere human teaching and the influence of the environment in which it grew. But how is it, if the germ had in it the truth, that it lost its hold over some of the greatest minds of the early centuries? If Dr. Fairbairn makes the teaching of the Church responsible for the anti-Christian character of the French revolution, he must apply the same reasoning to the teaching of the apostles in the first century of Christianity—and that teaching must itself be responsible for the easy corruption of Christianity which began to take place so soon in the first ages for the Church. But if that teaching itself was to blame then, in accordance with this reasoning, the ultimate responsibility must rest with Christ Himself.

If, again, it was to the fact that the germ was left to the influence of its environment and the distortions of human reason that Christianity so soon became corrupt—what are we to say of Dr. Fairbairn's belief in human reason as opposed to Newman's distrust of it? Who is trusting most to human reason here—Newman, who considers that the germ, containing truth and a great and deep idea, could be safely left to the environment of human reason and the protection of Providence, or Dr. Fairbairn, who considers that it must inevitably have been distorted?—Newman, who believes that human reason brought truth to truth and aided in the development of the Christian Idea, (though only in one set of its aspects after another), or Dr. Fairbairn, who thinks that human reason failed to recognize the truth as it really was, overlaid it by accretions of its own, did not bring truth to truth, but modified, stunted, tortured, and twisted it out of all recognition—till men might be excused for turning away from it as, on the whole, more false than true? If it is suicidal for Newman to distrust the reason in the individual, why is it not suicidal for Dr. Fairbairn to distrust the reason in the mass? But, as Dr. Fairbairn ought surely to allow, Newman does not make an absolute claim for reason even in the development of the Church. He does not deny that there are eternal ideas or that man, in the long run, is ruled by them; but Dr. Fairbairn blames him for saying that these ideas are " not sufficiently commanding for public union and action," as giving too small a power to ideas. But Newman is inclined to allow more power to ideas which are true and are protected by the providence of God than Dr. Fairbairn, for he considers that, by its intrinsic power and the protection of God, the germ idea of Christianity probably survived, absorbed, transcended and made use of the influences which came to it from without and is present now in the Christian Church.

He does not, however, pretend that the Church so far changed human nature as to make ideas of themselves sufficiently commanding for public union and action. He is ready to admit, as he does expressly admit, that the Popes have not always stirred up the Divine gift which is within them. He is ready to admit that this treasure is in earthen vessels. It may be true, then, that for the loss of a great part of Christendom and for the failure to gain so large a part of the world the Church is chiefly responsible. The Church may have made too absolute a claim for the truth she held; may have asserted her authority too much as from above, too little as connatural to, and in consonance with, the human reason. It may have been—indeed, few Catholics will deny that it was —the obscurantism of ecclesiastics which lost to

the Church the vigorous French intellect of the
18th century. No modern Catholic historian
worth mentioning will deny that it was, to a great
extent, the laxity of churchmen which lost to the
Church the rugged intellect of the reformers.
Nay, even in the early Church, Newman does not
deny that many a heretic was condemned for the
premature utterance of what turned out afterwards
to be true, and it is possible that Newman would
admit, in these cases as he certainly does in others,
that such heretics might sometimes have been
treated more leniently and that authority was
sometimes as much to blame for precipitating a
heresy as the heretic for incurring it.

He goes further than this. He allows that
heretics sometimes argued with better logic,
with more patience, courtesy and enlighten-
ment than their orthodox opponents. There has
been abundant waste, as in nature, so in the
Church, in the preservation of the type. There
has been inevitable disaster here and there. There
has been unnecessary disaster over and over again
—and the question where the personal responsibility must rest cannot be answered till the end of
time. But all this does not touch Newman's main
contention, that, in spite of incidental corruption
and ecclesiastical tyranny, the Church has preserved the type and represented Christian
consciousness in the main, has never let drop the
reality of Christian teaching, has not allowed it to
be explained away, has represented, age after age,
in the fullest and richest and most complex form

we can hope to get, one set of aspects after another, of the Christian idea; harmonized them and set them forth as a consistent whole in a manner which no other Christian community has dared to do; while reconciling and assimilating masses of religious thought from every age and from every quarter.

None of the admissions which have been made touch the contention that it is in the main stream of Christian tradition that the Christian idea is still most harmoniously and most richly,—though not yet completely, expressed, and where it may alone be finally realized—partly because it *is* the main stream and because there has been no break in its continuity.

And so Newman would argue, that even if the Papacy be but a crude and approximate centre of unity and means of expressing that "unity in multitude" which Pascal found essential to the Christian Church, yet it is only here that man will ultimately be able to find the basis for a complete and organic development of Christianity.

It is here—where the "whole pell mell of human life" is to be found and the greatest attempt to reconcile opposites has been made and the richest realization of the Christian type has been possible;—and not in the efforts of any individual;—that the Ideal Christ and the Idea that can only come through Him, must be realized.

(8)

In connection with Dr. Fairbairn's indictment of Newman we may, then, answer the questions which we drew out in the first chapter as to the main position of Newman (which so closely resembles that of Pascal) in the following manner.

How, it was asked, does Newman, from the premisses of scepticism come to the conclusions of faith ? If he considers that the conclusions depend upon the right use of the reason, how does he find what is the right use of the reason ?

It is on the perception that, for the individual and for the race, man must be considered as one and that the truth for which man makes is one, that the right use of the reason depends. It is by the use of what Newman called the " illative sense "— which brings "the whole man " to the task of making for truth; it is by the perception that action as well as thought takes part in the pursuit of truth; it is by the perception that it is only in the complete realization of type both in the individual and in the mass—in variety and in unity— that any proposition becomes realized so as to be " true " for the whole man or for the whole race.

It is conceivable that the ideas so realized are not true; that there is a reality which mocks the whole endeavour of man; but this is to make an arbitrary and gratuitous assumption—and the invention of such a reality—far beyond the scope of man's endeavour, may but be owing to the pathetic realization of the fact—that for no individual, for no generation, but only for the race,—

and then only in aspect after aspect, immanently and not in its transcendant completeness, can the truth be known as it lies in the bosom of the Eternal. In comparison with its completeness all aspects of it may seem but poor and barren, all representations of it but feeble and immature—all its moralities but convention—all its law but a provocation to sin. But here the religious sense, with its great representatives in the conscience of man, in its special types, in the great religious races, has come to the redemption and consolation of man. The religious sense which is the elementary capacity for the recognition of law in the nature of man—to which morality itself may possibly owe its birth—goes beyond morality and the statical reason, and finds in the narrowness of all known law; in the insufficiency of all aspects and representations of truth; in the crudity of all discovered moralities—not a reason for despair, but a basis for hope. The very fact that man has this discontent with his law, his moralities, his representations of truth shows that he has a capacity for a truth more complete and that in breaking through a narrower law he may be finding his way to a higher and a deeper; a law which will ultimately reconcile the contradictions of his nature—the law which created him and made him what he is.

The complex differentiation of function, which has resulted from the evolution of man's brain and intellect, has been the cause of that separation of the reason and the religious sense or the conscience

—with which Dr. Fairbairn is so much perplexed in Newman's treatment of the subject. The separation of the moral sense from the religious sense may perplex Dr. Fairbairn still more, but its cause also lies in the differentiation of function which time makes ever clearer and more necessary.

But Newman did not separate these faculties in order to isolate, but in order to combine, and if Dr. Fairbairn had understood Newman's treatment of the illative sense he would have understood the nature of this combination. In order that man may be himself, he must realize his type; but his realization of his type is only possible when all his faculties are combined and acted on as belonging to a whole. In order that the religious idea may be itself, it must realize its type, but the realization of its type is only possible when man has become one and has combined in a Catholic organism. The great office of religion;—as it has been (as Newman considers) that which gave birth to the moral sense; is ultimately to become the means by which humanity is to acquire full consciousness of itself and both to set the individual at unity with himself and the race at unity with the laws of its being. It is the religious sense which (as Newman conceives it) set man making the great experiment by which these laws may be discovered; because it was the religious sense which presented such a discovery as possible and made man's discontent a reason for hope instead of a reason for despair.

With Newman, then, the satisfaction of man's

aspiration for the ideal should not begin with the question whether God is knowable, but with the question whether there is a religion for man. The question is not concerned with what man's knowledge—considered as finite and expressed in words, has been able to possess itself of and acquire; but what he has done with his thought, which is infinite. It is here, if anywhere, that there is any hope of finding whether man has or has not any necessary relation to what he calls God and worships.

(9)

In the next chapter—where we shall consider in what sense and at what point Newman ceased to be a traditionalist we shall be concerned with the inner answer to the questions here considered. The misapprehension of Newman's argument is so complete in Dr. Fairbairn and in those who before Dr. Fairbairn have taken up a similar position that in discussing their objections we find ourselves insensibly carried far away from the thesis with which Newman was really concerned. It may be asked, then, how so complete a misapprehension of a writer who, as Dr. Hort considers, has a genius for lucidity beyond almost any writer in history, should be possible?

I think the answer is that the blame lies partly with Newman himself and partly with his opponents. Newman's dislike of pedantry induced him to set on one side terminology which is almost necessary to the discussion of the problems he put before him ; and, if it may be pleaded in his excuse that his writings are occasional and that he was bound to use popular language, this excuse will hardly avail for the " Grammar of Assent " which begins as a treatise and ends as a piece of popular apologetics.   Dr. Fairbairn is thus able to use the common language of modern philosophy and contend that Newman, with his delicate eighteenth century style, fails to find an equivalent in expression for the problem he has got to solve. With all Newman's lucidity therefore, it is possible to make quotation after quotation which seems to imply the sort of absoluteness it was Newman's main endeavour to destroy.   When we understand how much in the " Grammar of Assent " is written for the purpose of undermining scholasticism this misapprehension becomes impossible.

On the other hand, Newman's opponents, one and all, cannot rid themselves of the ordinary Protestant notion that in Newman, as with some Catholic writers, the principle of authority is something final and a short cut to the solution of religious problems.   It was the aim of the " Grammar of Assent " to show that this is not so.

(4.)—NEWMAN AS MYSTIC.

THE INTERIOR ARGUMENT OF NEWMAN AND PASCAL.

It is not true either of Pascal or of Newman (as has been too commonly supposed) that they abandoned rational metaphysic for a purely traditionalist theory of religion. They do not, indeed, deal immediately with metaphysic; but their peculiar use of the traditional argument differs from Traditionalism in this: that it is founded on the unity of a universal law. Pascal had discovered, as we learn from a single sentence in his Pensées, the possible beginning of moral law and of nature itself in what is scarcely less than a prophetic description of evolution; and Newman had found the meaning and value of religious tradition in a law of development which makes for the survival of the fittest in ideas as evolution in the life of nature.

" If habit is a second nature," says Pascal; " perhaps Nature is a first habit."

" To live is to change," says Newman carrying on this conception of development, " and to be perfect is to have changed often."

This constant onward journey of nature and the human race, though it is not at all times clearly taught by either Pascal or Newman, is constantly implied by both of them; and is based on the immanental conception of the Divine in " the original constitution of man,"—which alone can account at once for his greatness and his misery; for the steady and unchanging consistency and growth of his religious hopes, his ever-increasing consciousness of his limitations; the slowly emerging unity of the moral law; the dignity acquired ever more completely by man as he becomes more and more conscious, though he be but a " reed " in the Universe, of the unity and progress of his thought.

The greatness of man consists in his thought; the greatness of thought in its unity—the unity which it is able to acquire within, and the unity which it is able to establish without, the man who thinks.

But in that man is, at the same time, the frailest of creatures and but an atom in the universe, his very greatness is to him a source of misery; and, if the greatness of his thought consists in the unity which it can attain, it leads him from that very attainment, to suspect the existence of a unity beyond him which is altogether unattainable. Were there any clear proof that God existed then might man be satisfied; were there any certainty that God did not exist, man might be content; but now that there is enough to set him on the search but not enough to assure him that he has been successful in it, he is driven to and fro in a hopeless quest and ever recurring misery.

Man is great because he seeks for God, and miserable because he cannot find him.   And here Pascal finds that antimony of the nature of man which throws him alternately into scepticism and dogmatism, into Agnosticism and Gnosticism. But Pascal replies to both Dogmatist and Sceptic that man's misery and greatness point alike to the existence of the transcendent Unity of which they are in search or in despair of finding which they fall into misery.   He replies alike to Humanity and to the solitary seeker after God—" In that thou hadst sought, thou hadst already found."   The desire could not have grown up in a Universe, whether constantly evolving or created, in which there was nothing to respond to it; the hope could not spring up in a heart which was complete or could be at rest without the Divine; the search could not have been begun had not man already been compelled, by an exigency of his nature, to recognize both that there was a way and that there was a goal.

(1.)

But it is supposed that Newman and Pascal by the very fact of throwing man upon the religious tradition and demanding that he shall forego a speculative argument for God, are " vilifying " reason, become inconsistent with their own speculative position and commit themselves either to a fatal incoherency of thought or else to a scepticism from which they can only be rescued by an arbitrary faith.* This misapprehension arises from the fact that men are " always for precipitating things "; that they will not take the arguments one by one but invariably expect that the whole argument, especially the whole argument for religion, shall be stated at once.

In the method which they adopt, Pascal and Newman, addressing themselves to men of the world and not to philosophers, were forced, in the first place, to deal with the concrete and were building up an external argument from an external unity in religious thought; but, in so doing they were making the way clear for the argument from that internal unity of which the external is a result and, when it is shown to exist, a proof.

To this internal unity, both for Pascal and for Newman, the inconsistency or the despair of the reason when left to itself, is a testimony; because there could not be despair had there not been the hope, nor the hope had there not been a prior unity in thought to inspire it.

I have already observed that Newman's conception of a tradition in religion did not include the notion (as it did with the Traditionalists) of a primitive revelation. Nor does that of Pascal. It is based on the internal revelation made to man by the exigencies of his nature in his battle with circumstance; in his attempt to discover what was suitable or necessary to that nature as a whole; in his endeavour to gain for himself his true environment, in thought and ideas as well as in fact and

* Some form of Mysticism.

K

in action.   It was based on the unity of thought
and the consistency of direction which was to be
found in the religious experience of man.

If, then, Newman admits that there are
opposite certitudes, and that certitude, in the
individual, is no test of truth, he is rescued from
the deadlock to which his adversaries consider him
reduced, by that criterion of the sanity or insanity,
the wisdom or folly, of certitude, which he found
in the social and historical development of man.
Those certitudes which survive and which can be
tested dynamically as well as statically; those
certitudes which are found to belong " to the whole
man " and to be something more than the result of
special operations of the intellect or the feelings,
by the testimony of history and their power to
build up civilizations, to develop and to grow as
well as to survive;—those certitudes are, indeed,
tests of truth.   Aristotle holds no opinion to have
become " certainty " until it can be said to reach
to the greatest depth of our being.   That which
reaches the greatest depth of the being of man,
under all circumstances, and in all time, belongs to
the ultimate unity of his thought.   It was to the
sum and assimilated mass of religious experience
(so far as time has enabled man to find it) as well
as to the consistency, and fertility of its developments—its power to survive the thought that was
opposed to it, its power to preserve its original
type—that Newman yielded his assent when he
entered the Catholic Church.   In its attempt to
secure the unity of human thought in religion

Newman finds the most general argument for the Church; because that opinion or belief which can stand the test of the greatest number of the states of our being is that which alone can have reached the greatest depths of being with which man is, as yet, acquainted. To the sum of religious thought in all the world as well as to its most consistent presentation in its modern form, I repeat, did Newman consider he yielded his assent on entering the Catholic Church; for he speaks, in a famous passage, of the Church as like the Divine child, sitting in the midst of the Doctors of Pagan thought and Gentile religion, both hearing them and asking them questions; and in its power to assimilate religious thought and religious practice from without, in all ages and in all lands, he finds one of the tests of the vitality and growth of the religious organism. The Child conceived as man was actually in ignorance and was then beginning to form for Himself that thought which through His teaching has gained so singular a sway in the world. The Child, con- ceived as the God of that Humanity which is finding its unity through Him, was bringing into a Divine coherence the elements of religious truth that lay scattered and isolated, in all parts of the world and among all conditions of men.

Now the great writers, on the Protestant side, do not deny the value and meaning of unity. All thought which progresses at all, if it arrives at any truth, must arrive at a certain consistency and must become at unity with itself. All thought, in every department of life, is making for and attempting a unity. This they admit. But they deny that the Catholic Church presents us with a true unity. They say that it is, for the most part, an external uniformity brought about by coercion.

It is considered, therefore, that Pascal and Newman have recourse to the external unity of the Catholic Church because they are inwardly sceptical, and deny the power of man's reason to attain to unity except through the means of coercion and authority.

But this is not true of Newman or of Pascal or of the Church, but only of the "Traditionalism" which the Church has condemned.

The objection to Traditionalism is that it shuts up man's conception of God in the notion of a Primitive Revelation, and makes man dependent, for his religion, upon a revelation from without rather than upon the objective validity of his religious thought gained from the knowledge of its practical universality.

It, therefore, tends to make man find his spiritual freedom in the service of the Church which gives him the tradition rather than in the service of God to Whom that tradition testifies. It has the effect, which has been observed wherever it has prevailed, whether in the Catholic or Protestant Churches (for it has, at times, prevailed in both) of making men cultivate obedience at the expense of originality; of encouraging general servitude of the mind rather than that kind of service which is itself man's perfect freedom and of checking the progress of the very religion to which it owes its existence.

And in this way, traditionalism came into direct opposition to the religious tradition itself. For, in its Christian form, this tradition testifies to the fact that man has a law *within* him which differentiates right from wrong, " his conscience accusing or else excusing " and a power *within* him of seeking after God in which lies the very meaning of man's belief in the Divine. Man, indeed, receives the object of his religious nature from without and by means of tradition and through other men; but not only is the evolution of this religious nature, which calls for such an object, conceived by the religious tradition as springing up from within man at the beginning; but in every generation the whole process starts again from the beginning in every individual.

Every man is bidden by that tradition to seek and to find for himself the God which it presents to him.

Moreover, it is in man's power to change and to deepen his conception of God that the strongest proof of the progressive unity of his thought resides. The depth and plausibility of modern Agnosticism is only negative proof of the existence in man of this power to develop and to enlarge his religion. The religious tradition, then, is conceived by the Church as absorbing and taking up into itself all the affirmative results of the ever renewed struggle of man's soul in his search for the unity of his thought, in every generation and in every individual; whereas traditionalism conceives of the existence of God as a definite external fact, revealed once for all to man from wtihout, and having nothing to do with the development of man's religious sense from within or that immanental revelation which is the only revelation to which history can testify.

If we now return to Pascal we shall find that this line of thought was familiar to him. The external unity of the Church is prior, in his mind, to the coercion which attempts to preserve it, and is itself the result of an interior unity in the thought of man of which it is the best evidence and the clearest proof. There is coercion; and coercion has been pressed to an extreme; but it is coercion in the name of consistency, of growth and of interior unity. It has sometimes gone so far (we now commonly perceive) as to prevent the very growth, and to endanger the very unity of thought in whose behalf it was said to be employed. But it was not prior to the unity; it was not the cause of the unity; which actually exists.

It was a protest on behalf of the whole against the part; it was the protest of man taken as a moral, religious and social, as well as an intellectual, being, against speculations which regarded him under one aspect alone. It was a protest in favour of social and religious unity, as necessary to the " wholeness " even of the individual, against the individualism which would break it up into sectarianism, provincialism or nationalism. It was a protest in favour of what had been found

suitable to the whole nature of man, against private
and particular conceptions, which would shut him
up in one period of his thought or in a single form
of his activity.

It will be found that in their attitude towards
reason and speculation in the individual and in the
mass Burke, Pascal and Newman are remarkably
in agreement.   The unity of human thought is,
for each, to be found in the mass.   Neither
one nor the other vilifies the intellect; but
all alike question the validity of its testimony when
it stands alone; whether in the individual as
opposed to the race or in the name of a particular
faculty as opposed to the unity of the whole man.
When Burke speaks of what is suitable to the
whole nature of man and opposes this to theories of
individuals which do but answer to one part of
his being, he appeals to that kind of expedience
which has been found by experience to set man at
unity with himself.   He appeals on behalf of
reason in the mass against particular theory and
speculation.   He does not, he says, condemn
theory or speculation, because that would be to
vilify reason itself; but he requires of such theory
or speculation that it should first reckon with
reason in the mass and be submitted to the touch-
stone of experience in that region political or
religious with which the theory or speculation is
concerned; because that experience, in politics and
religion (which have an immediate practical
bearing) shows the results, and testifies to the
unity, of the reason of man exercised on the largest

scale and connected with the greatest number of the states of man's being which we can bring to bear on the subject in question.

When Newman speaks of eternal ideas as discoverable by man but as not sufficiently commanding to be made a basis for common union and action, he means that men are commonly incapable of ideas if they are to be discovered by speculation and by theory, and that only *such ideas* as are presented by means of religion so as to bring unity into all the processes of man's life and so as to be suitable to his whole nature and to all the states of it, are in a position to command, because they alone admit of a practical as well as an intellectual test; they alone can be submitted to the test of a long experience and the deeper expediency; and they alone can give to men (taken in the mass) any chance of unity in thought or consistency in action. What the man of genius or the philosopher may discover by the immediate action of his intellect, the human race discovers by experiment, by action, by the slow processes of experience; and, while the man of genius has made his discovery only on the lines of intellect, the human race finds for the truth discovered a basis broader and more secure by finding its relation to all the exigencies of man's being and all the conditions of his feelings.

Both the philosopher and the race of which he forms a part are making for, and express, the unity of man's thought; but the race can do what the philosopher cannot, can find by experience how

the whole being of man is a result of unity profounder still—a unity of which the unity of thought
is but a particular expression.   It is in the unity
of man's moral and spiritual as well as his intellectual being; it is in the fact that a certain
external and voluntary unity in these things has
been attainable by man—and is ever more and
more to be attained—that is to be found the first
and most easily recognizable testimony to the
absolute unity of the Universe in which man's
being is assumed by the Church to be founded.

By making this experiment on this assumption, man has found one of the ways of discovering
whether the assumption is true.   His progress, his
civilization as well as his religious unity (though
all three are yet far from the ideal attainment) are
yet each of them strong testimony to the truth of
the assumption; for they show a unity gained
amid the greatest difference yet known to man; a
unity between races opposed by temperament, by
blood and by temper more than any races that have
had any unity at all before; a unity of a greater
variety of races; and a unity (where it is attained)
more remarkable than any heretofore experienced
because it is deeper, more complex and
more inward and has met with a
greater number of streams of tendency in opposite
directions than the unities attained on so stupendous scale (from similar causes and with a similar
testimony to the unity at the base of things) in
India, China, and among Oriental races generally.

It is not, then, reason in the great mass of

men; it is not reason where it represents and
attempts to unify the whole of man's experience; it
is not thought contemplated as one great whole
against which Burke or Newman make any protest,
—but the intellect of the individual attempting to
found in terms of the intellect alone a basis for
that human nature which is still on its way to
completeness and with which the intellect may not
even yet be completely acquainted.

For if there is already to be found in the world
an immanental unity, not less certain is it that
there is, in the future, a unity which transcends it.
The sciences could not exist without this unity in
the past; but all scientific men are agreed that this
is nothing to the progress and systematization
which must happen in the future. But this
progress and systematization are nothing else but
a tendency to, and a realization of, a unity even
more complex, even more remarkable, even more
extended in its sway.

When Pascal, too, speaks of thought as that
which confers dignity and greatness on man but
at the same time uses expressions of despair about
the limitations of man's reason; when he exalts
man's power to seek, but mourns his inability to
find, the unity of the universe; he is no more inconsistent with himself than are Burke and Newman.

Thought it is which has given to man the very
conception of any unity at all. But thought alone
cannot find, and by itself, would not even seek, that
unity whose discovery is dependent upon a motive
derived from the dynamics of man's nature.

" The heart has reasons that the reason knows not of," and it is the heart that adds an impulse to the intellect ere it can search with unwearied patience and in the very fact of searching find.

Reason by itself; reason without the emotions; reason, taken as intellect, and not representing the whole man, would rest satisfied before the whole nature of the unity it seeks was discovered; for the intellect in isolation demands unity indeed but not absolute unity,—not a unity which shall satisfy heart as well as mind.   Not until the intellect has learnt to understand and to represent the whole man does this absolute unity appear to it, what in fact it then becomes, an intellectual as well as a religious and moral necessity.

Nevertheless, the reply of Pascal, if we examine it in the light of what has now been said, is an answer to the reason as well as to the religious sense.   We may sum up Pascal's account of the sceptical side of man's nature in the answer which it gives to the question " Can man by searching find out God ?"   The sceptical side of man answers " No."

We may sum up the dogmatic side of man's nature by its answer to the same question; for it answers " Yes."

But Pascal says that both are right and both are wrong.

By no direct speculative argument can man arrive at the absolute or the infinite; and therefore the dogmatist is wrong.   He must first assume the very thing he wants to prove.

But man does seek for the absolute and the infinite and could not do so if he were not already aware that there was something to be sought; were he not aware of some privation of what must in some sense also he his.   He could not discover or invent an exigency of his nature which did not belong to it prior to all thought and before he had begun to enquire.   And, therefore, the sceptic also is wrong, for he must deny, not only that the search can be successful, but that it could ever have been begun.

To both, to all, to Humanity at large and to the individual, Pascal makes God reply " In that thou hadst sought Me, thou hadst already found Me."

It is the answer of the unity of man's thought to all his particular thinking; it is the answer of the unity of the Universe to all particular investigation; it is the answer of absolute unity to all thought, to all enquiry and to all prayer.

And as it is the answer to these; so is it the sole justification for all thought, for all enquiry, for all prayer.

Were not the universe based on an absolute unity not only would all prayer be vain (for there would be no unity higher or deeper than man's, the most complex and the latest unity the universe has developed, with which he could unite himself), but all inquiry would be useless and all thought impossible.   Two intelligible words spoken by a child are the result of a tendency to unity at which it has taken that tendency billions of years to arrive; but the earliest expression of that tendency could not have existed did it not answer to the nature of the Universe itself. No number of instances, however great, proves an absolute unity but all these instances prove the taking for granted such a unity in the process of things before any consciousness of unity was possible.

Now in arguing at all, the sceptic is compelled to assume the objective unity of thought, and in admitting the progressive unity of the sciences he is compelled to admit the practical universality of this unity. Here, then, an objective unity has been borne within the subjective consciousness. The only assertion left for the sceptic is that it may be an illusion, and that therefore all certitude remains impossible.

But we have only found out that there is such a thing as illusion by comparing it with this objective unity. Without this objective unity we should have no conception of the meaning of illusion. It is only then by arbitrarily assuming the possible existence of a reality more real than the only reality we know that the sceptic can justify his suspicion that this reality is an illusion.

The sceptic has a right to his position simply because it is possible to thought; nor is scepticism without a place in the history of religion. It points to the necessary limitations of our faculty and proves that we cannot include the whole of possibility in any conceivable system.

It is, at this point, that Newman and Pascal part company altogether with the dogmatist,

though they cannot be said to join with the sceptic.
The dogmatist, indeed, admits the possibility of
doubt in words but seems to deny it in fact. But
the difference between Pascal and Newman on one
side and the sceptic on the other is that the sceptic
considers possibility a sufficient reason for practical
doubt whether the speculative unity is valid at all;
whereas Newman and Pascal consider it sufficient
only to prove a limitation of our faculties.   And
this limitation does not prove that the absolute
unity, for which these faculties seek, does not exist;
but, that it is not to be found in subject alone or
without it alone, but in that unity which is called
absolute only because it completely unites two
kinds of reality into one.

The doubt is sufficient to prove a mystery but
not to demonstrate illusion; to make God incom-
prehensible but not to make Him unknowable; to
make the ultimate unity of man's thought only
partially attainable by man but not to remove the
fact of an ultimate unity (pre-supposed in the
totality of man's being) from his nature as the only
object for which he can employ those energies
which most differentiate him from the brutes; the
only environment in which the most distinctive
part of his developed being can exist at all.

Now it is on the unity of the moral being of
man and the unity of the religious element within
him that Newman lays most stress.

To this element in man it is in the first place
that Pascal addresses the Divine words "Thou
hadst not sought Me, hadst thou not already found

Me." It is, in the first place, an answer to the solitary seeker after God, and, only in the next, the answer of the unity of the Universe to all the inquiry and all the thoughts of man.

And it is the religious element in man which first set him seeking not merely for an ideal life nor only for the ideal, but for a law that should be absolute and a unity which should transcend and should absorb all the unities of life.

Conscience, as Newman conceives it, is not a law but a feeling for a law; not the dictate of a law-giver but the consciousness that there is a law—a unity in the moral being of man like, but transcending, the unity of his thought in other things. It is not a testimony to the existence of a uniform, moral law throughout the world of men, for its testimony is inconsistent and one kind of moral law is held the true one here and another there. But it began, whenever it began, as a sense that a law there is. And in seeking it had already begun to find,—not indeed the perfect law of liberty —but yet a law of some sort, suitable to its condition, tentative and hypothetical in fact but peremptory and stern enough in its dictates.

Throw back the argument which Newman uses for the Church, on the basis of development, and apply it to the slowly emerging sense of morality and religion and we shall find that the development of the conscience was altogether similar to the development of the Church. The gradual attainment of unity in the moral being of man, because he unconsciously started on a single inevitable line of orientation till he discovered the notion of right and wrong and could give his new consciousness a name; with all the difficulties he encountered; with all the inconsistencies into which he fell, with all the comparisons of tradition with tradition which occurred as one race came into contact with another; with all the various stages of development through which he passed; is, in every respect, parallel, to the slow development and complex unity of the religious idea in the Christian Church—a culminating point and continuation of the history of conscience in the world.

Newman, strangely enough, never explicitly accepted the principle of evolution in man, though he probably held it in some form peculiar to himself. But so far from there being any inconsistency between his conception of religion and the doctrine of evolution, one can hardly be said to be consistent without the other.

The moral certitudes, slowly gained by the conscience of man, are parallel to the religious certitudes, slowly developed by the Church; admit of the same tests, are liable to the same corruption, are proved sane or insane, suitable or unsuitable to the whole nature of man, by the same method.

And, as nature testifies to the absolute unity of the Universe in which she lies, so man also adds, in his complex moral development, one more testimony to that unity of which it is but an ever clearer result, an ever profounder symbol, an ever deepening proof.

This, then, is the interior argument for

judging by their survival or decay, their growth or decline, of the sanity or insanity of those religious certitudes upon which the great religious tradition of humanity is founded.

It is only when seen in the mass and in this complete social aspect; it is only when they have received the confirmation of centuries and of progress that the fact of their being a food to humanity and not a poison, at unity with the whole nature of man, expedient to the unity of his thought and to his unity with himself and inspiring to his organic development, that these certitudes (so often opposed in their expression when contemplated in isolation) no longer lead to that deadlock which arises from contradiction, but point to the fact that they are founded on a Unity which must go on, for all time, increasing their intensity and enlarging their scope.

The Church, then, thus regarded, began with the beginning of conscience; has developed in accordance with the same law and claims the allegiance of man on the same title. It is, as a society, heir by default to all that the conscience and religious element in man have been able to acquire, on a social basis, consistently with his intellectual and scientific progress.

But it is also more than this. It testifies by its unity and by its development alike to the unity of the religious thought of man and to the absolute unity to belief in which it owes its existence; whose reality is an article of its creed;

of whose universal sway it is at once a representative, an instance and an exponent.

" In that thou hadst sought, thou hadst already found."

I have said that these words are addressed first to the solitary seeker after God and only in the second place tō that Humanity which has been seeking God ever since it has appeared on the stage of history. And in these words may be found the reconciliation between the individualistic and the social conception of religion.

" Woe unto him that is alone," says Lamennais, the great champion of Traditionalism. " Woe unto him that is alone;" says he to the solitary seeker after God; for, though he seek Him, he shall never find Him. From the great tradition of the human family alone can the Divine idea be learned, for from that testimony alone can man become assured of the validity of his thought; from the universality of its subjective certitudes or aspirations alone can their objective validity be proved; from a revelation made to Humanity at the beginning witnessed to by all the races of mankind and summed up and delivered to the individual by the Church—from such a tradition alone can man learn the articles of his creed. In this Traditionalism, condemned by the Pope, so thoughtful a writer as Tulloch finds the essence of Popery.

And yet most philosophers will allow, and Tulloch himself among them, that it is from the universality of the subjective laws of thought that their objective validity is proved, if it can be proved at all.

And here it can scarcely be denied that Traditionalists were right, if they were not to fall into the scepticism which would deny that there is any objective validity in thought.

Why then were Traditionalists condemned?

There can, indeed, be little doubt that they were condemned too soon and in too peremptory a manner; nor do the advocates of the Papacy deny that Lamennais, their leader, was treated with a harshness and intolerance which amounted to little less than persecution. But, nevertheless, the Church had been thinking out the problem for many centuries before Lamennais appeared and had come to a conclusion not dissimilar to that which Tulloch expresses when he calls Traditionalism the essence of Popery. With Popery itself, perhaps, Tulloch was not very intimately acquainted; but he means that Traditionalism would lead at once to ecclesiastical tyranny and would destroy the religious liberty of the individual for ever. He means that in so far as the Church can be proved to have exercised an ecclesiastical tyranny, it was on a Traditionalistic basis that she had done so.

Yet it remains a fact that though the Church like other religious institutions, has sometimes fallen into Traditionalism, she has never explicitly committed herself to its teaching. And now she has explicitly condemned it.

Tulloch, then, may be right (and I think I can

show that he is) in saying that Traditionalism leads to tyranny and that wherever the Church exercised an ecclesiastical tyranny she did so on an unconsciously traditionalistic basis. He may be right in so saying and we may admit that he is right not only without coming into opposition with the explicit teaching of the Church but in full and perfect consonance with that teaching.

The Church condemned Traditionalism because it denied that man, as an individual and apart from Revelation, could arrive at the belief in God. The belief in God or the Divine is the basis of all religion. He who takes away the power of the individual to arrive at a belief in God, takes away his power to originate in religion at all, or so diminishes his power as to leave him helpless in the face of the Tradition which surrounds him and has given him the basis of the religion which he holds. Traditionalism, therefore, would seem to tend as a theory, to destroy originality and the religious liberty of man.

Universality is, indeed, the completest proof we have of the validity of our subjective reasoning; and the Church attempts to apply that test on as large a scale as is possible. But reasoning may be valid and may be universally true without having yet gained the assent of all mankind. Religious reasoning may be valid and may be universally true without having gained the assent of all religious persons. And the individual, apart from tradition, may have arrived at a basis for religion on grounds which he might justly consider enough because he had no more. He might find, that is, something which answered sufficiently to the religious exigency of his nature to give him an object and to make life endurable. This would be his God and it would be his representation of what religion means by God.

The supposition of a being entirely solitary is necessary to explain the position, because the first directly conscious thought of religion must have occurred to an individual. It is necessary to conceive that any conscious being, even in complete solitude, might become aware of the religious exigencies of his nature and might supply them up to a certain point, from the very fact that he had found them.

The fact that he felt the need would present to him at once the nature of its satisfaction. In other words, *the fact that he was seeking would itself shew him that he had found.*

Such a being is ideal; because a man entirely solitary from his birth could scarcely be said to be capable of thought. But it illustrates the fact on which Pascal and the Church are relying that man (whether consciously or unconsciously) becomes satisfied of certain facts for himself; believes himself to be objective because he cannot help being aware of his own subjectivity and finds a test of the truth of his operations in the fact of his being compelled to live in accordance with them. His life is for him a test of truth. He can bring no objective test beyond his own belief in his objectivity to bear upon his operations; but he believes in them because he has no other test and cannot live without them.

The Church, then, makes room for the reality and the depth and the truth of the arguments for a God that occur apart from her own tradition. She holds that, among her own people, the belief in God or the Divine or whatever else it is that the tradition presents to the individual, does not spring from the tradition alone or the authority of the Church, but also from an exigency of man's nature which would have demanded, sooner or later, something of this kind, whether it had been presented or not.

Tradition of some sort there must be, even in order that man should think; for words themselves come to man by a tradition. But words must have come into existence to serve the purposes of something very near to thought—that inchoate thought in which feeling first attempted to express itself. In this sense thought is prior to words. The Church, then, holds that the basis of religion does not rest on authority alone, on revelation alone or on tradition alone; but upon tradition as united with an exigency in the heart and intellect of the man who receives it. And as the tradition contributes something to the man who receives it, so he, too, is able to contribute something to the tradition which he receives. On this basis rests his power to originate in religious thought, and on this basis rests his religious liberty. And this religious liberty of the individual the Church proclaimed in her condemnation of Traditionalism.

Though it is commonly allowed that Lamennais was, in one sense, a representative of religious liberty, and Gregory XVI. in the same sense, a representative of religious tyranny when he condemned him; yet, in another and far deeper sense, the Pope, however, peremptory and premature his condemnation may have been, was, on this occasion the true champion of the liberty of mankind.

Still, without doubt, he acted despotically; and, strangely enough, the crude condemnation of Traditionalism may be taken as an instance of the Church's falling into the very error she condemned. For she fell into that arbitrary and mechanical mode of regarding tradition which allows no time for originality to mature; and thus refused to recognize that liberty in the individual which is logically necessary to her own position; because her tradition itself is dependent on the reason and on the free acceptance of fallible men.

It is necessary to make this perfectly clear because one of the ways in which Newman, and, through him, the Church has sometimes been attacked as sceptical, has been to say that he considers that a man can only come to believe in a God through the Church, or that a man could not believe in a God without believing in the Church. Whereas what he said was that a perfectly consistent mind which believed in a God would go on to believe in the Church.

(4)

I said some time ago that a popular religion would always be corrupt; that the Catholic Church represents a popular religion and that this popular religion is corrupt. If it is corrupt, then, it must have some characteristic vice; and its vice is superstition.

The exercise of authority in the Church is not always infallible, even in the opinion of Ultramontanes. If it is not always infallible, it may be, sometimes, tyrannous, despotic and peremptory. A popular religion has a vice and the authority, which represents it, may be expected to have some defect which is parallel to the vice of the popular religion.

In a Church, which has a powerful tradition, it might well be expected that, if it erred, it would err in making too arbitrary a use of its tradition. That is, its defect would be a tendency to fall into traditionalism. A Church, founded on the social as opposed to the individualistic idea, would have its defect in a tendency to exclude the individual. A Church which had aimed at systematization would have its defect in a tendency to exclude originality.

All these defects, in a certain degree and in temporary exhibitions of them, we may allow that authority in the Catholic Church has sometimes shown, without denying that an authority it is.

But, in the main and by her real teaching the Church holds a doctrine according to which the individual freely

receives and freely uses her tradition in
sincere accordance with the religious experience of
his own life. That is, she reconciles, in her
doctrine, the individualistic and social conceptions
of religion; though, in her practice, she has too
often sacrificed the individual for the Society. In
this sense, then, Tulloch is right when he said he
regarded Traditionalism as the essence of Popery.
When Church authority has fallen into traditionalism (a parallel defect to that of superstition
in the people), it has exhibited all that peremptori-
ness, all that tyranny, all that unwillingness to
give place to originality or to genius which
Protestants usually associate with the word
" Popery."

In her theory, then, the Church allows such
liberty to the individual as will make his testimony
to her truth equal to that of, at least, a unit in
humanity. So far as she has done so in fact, her
unity is real and significant.

Here, then, we may find an internal limit to
the coercive authority of the Church—a limit which
is part of the Church's teaching.

The individual is not regarded by the Church
merely as a passive receptacle for her tradition.
He accepts it, when he comes to years of discre-
tion, because it answers to an exigency of his
nature and he can only discover that it does so by
the use of his reason. Any hypothesis which, from
his own religious experience joined with the
tradition seems possible to a *bona fide* member of
the Catholic Society, however strange, however

original, however heterodox it may at first appear,
—if it be presented as a hypothesis only and as
long as it is not presented as a dogma—cannot be
justly condemned by authority until it is proved
to be false by the universal and certain consent of
mankind.

If the individual has the liberties of a unit in
a Society he may claim to be answered, if he
argues; to be refuted, if he makes hypotheses; but
as long as he does not usurp the rights of the
Society, as a whole, he may claim immunity from
condemnation. The error of Lamennais, then, and,
far more, the error of the modern Traditionalism
of conservative theologians consists in this: that,
while they allow for a logical development and for
such liberty in the individual as follows from it,
they do not sufficiently realize that the great
religious vision which the Church presents to
mankind owes its immediate validity to the free
testimony and active experience of the individuals
who have freely accepted it as in
accordance with the exigencies of their nature;
who have had experience of that vision,
though only in part; who can therefore,
each for himself, give some account of it,—not
indeed as if the particular vision were equal to the
whole,—but in accordance with special religious
opportunity and in terms free, fresh and original.
It is only in consequence of this liberty, too often
obscured and betrayed, that the Church has been
able to produce, not only social reformers and
saints, but the most strenuous individualists in

religion that the world can show—the vast host of
mystics, the followers of St. Theresa and St. John
of the Cross; not only Bossuet but Pascal; not
only St. Francis Xavier but Tauler; not only More
and Erasmus but Juliana of Norwich. Nothing
can exceed the freedom which has been claimed by
the mystics in the use of religious hypothesis.
The freedom, then, is granted by the Church in
theory, and must, in time, be granted, by the
Church's representatives, to criticism and history
as well as to mysticism.

From what has been said it will be obvious
that the certitudes at which man has arrived,
through the criterion offered by the Church, at one
period of his existence, will often appear crudely
expressed, at another period in which he is still
more mature; especially if any particular stream of
tendencies has borne him along a new line of
thought and opened to him new vistas of being.

But the certitudes, for all that, may not be the
less real or the less profound.   The more ridiculous his expressions for his consciousness of the
transcendental appear to him when his consciousness of the immanental is uppermost, the more his
inner nature is crying out for some new expressions of transcendence to redress its balance.

But to live from the greatest depth of our
being; to see that opposite desires may alike
deserve fruition; that the desire for finality and the

desire for growth; the desire for rest and the desire
for action; the desire to break down and the desire
to build; the desire to destroy and the desire to
preserve may, at all times, be rightly felt and justly
made motives of life—requires, above all things,
things, patience and courage.

Whether man be matter or spirit, certain it is
that he is suspended between two eternities and
that he knows it. Deep calls unto deep and the
breath of the upper and nether eternity,—the
eternity whence he comes, the eternity whither he
goes,—blows through his fragile being from the
day of his birth to his death. What can he
desire, then, with all the energies that being may
possess, but to be at one with that which begat him
and with that which shall, at last, receive him into
its arms? What is his hope but that he may have
peace and be at unity with these masters of his
destiny?

Whether he be matter or spirit he has desires;
and his main desire must ever be the explanation
and the underlying motive of all the desires he
knows. To be at one with himself; to be at one
with all the depths of his being; that he may rest
on the eternal that is below him and that he may
find room for all the complexity of his energy and
all the passionate yearning of his nature in the
eternity that is beyond him: this is the main
desire of man.

But his desires, taken one by one, are as
multitudinous and anarchical as they are pas-

sionate. How shall he reduce them to order and
so give them the best chance of fruition ? For he
sees very early in the course of his long journey
that the setting his desires in some kind of order is
essential to their having any fruition at all.

The ordering things by a certain standard,
the reducing of things to a certain unity, the
making the less give way to the greater, the
weaker to the stronger, the more superficial to the
more profound—these interior actions began in the
very animal or ever the animal conceived of itself
as man.

In the mere matter of his brain, whether
regarded as an expression of his spirit or as all that
there is of his thought, the great tradition of man's
intellectual unity began; and from this great
tradition it would be arbitrary to exclude, at any
point in its growth, however early, the conception
of that sense of order, that desire for unity, which is
represented by conscience.

And, indeed, conscience, as the desire for ultimate unity in morals, is the simplest of desires in
its origin. It represents the desire for order
unconnected with the thing to be set in order.
It belongs, therefore, to anything that can be said
to have desire; for, to all desire, a certain order is
essential, that it may meet with its fruition. This
must be done first and thus, in order that that may
be done next at all.

If man, then, has developed so far as not only
to have found a word for " being good at getting
this or that," but a word for " being good in

morals''; if he has got so far that this "being good in morals" he calls goodness *par excellence*, so that he has not to use any other word, but is immediately understood; this order and unity in him have travelled a long way and must have gone, in the main, in one direction. Here, then, a distinct line of orientation has been acquired; here is the matured judgment of the species on one great general point; and, in this line of orientation, he has found and made for himself a criterion—a criterion of right and wrong, a criterion of what is good and better and best in action.

"Goodness" then has stood, in its many forms, high enough in his esteem. It stands higher than anything else, for, if he thinks well of goodness in intellect he is compelled to add a second expression, but "goodness" is, however grotesque a form of it may present itself, a word which by itself has come to mean a special sort of being good at a thing, and means man's satisfaction in one kind of action only.

In the face of so stupendous a triumph of the moral nature of man, all the future victories in man's search for unity are as nothing. To have found, however vaguely, that there is a unity such as this is as much greater than anything afterwards attained as the discovery of number is greater than the discovery of algebra. And yet what follows is greater in this: that it is built on what has been already discovered and, if it stand, is a confirmation of all former discoveries.

Moreover, the sense of the malice of sin, the sense of moral responsibility, the fear of the Lord, the fear of some judgment to come or a judgment immediately to follow the deed, was the very characteristic of those religions which were regarded by men, who came to take a purely philosophical view of these matters, as superstitions. In this sense " fear made the gods " and fear was the parent of religion. But if the fear came first what created the fear? " No doubt, the dualism which man at once found in nature; the dualism which made nature his best friend and his most terrible enemy; the dualism which made him feel his intimate association and connection with the earth and the cruel necessity which compelled him to trust as his nearest ally one who invariably and inevitably at last betrayed him, crushed him to the earth and destroyed him. To primitive man the apparent dualism in things at once suggested an arbitrary being who changed his mind and repented that he had made man; or beings, some kindly and the others hostile, for ever interested in his career, watching his conduct and sometimes peering into his thoughts. Nevertheless, the process he was pursuing was a process of unification. He put together certain events as acts belonging to a particular kind of nature which he regarded as good. He put together another set of events as acts belonging to another

kind of nature which he regarded as evil. He
ordered; he classified; he unified; and the very
detection of difference was a means of advancing
to unity. It was a process of unification which led
to Polytheism as well as to Monotheism, and, as
soon as a single law underlying and connecting
the gods could be detected, the mind of man
rushed with the speed of light to the one God
who should be regarded as superior in power to
the rest.

The process of unification is, indeed, merely
the necessary course of the reasoning of man. He
cannot do otherwise, if he would, and, if he applies
his mind to what is called religion at all, he must
think in this way, for this is the very nature of
thinking.

If, then, the sceptic argues (as we all along
allow he may) that the necessity for an absolute
unity proved in the mind of man is no proof that
an absolute unity there is, St. Thomas as well as
Pascal and Newman reply that this argument may
overthrow the metaphysical dogmatist or it may
not; but it does not touch religion regarded as the
necessary relation of man to all his expressions for
God, the Divine, Infinity or Law. Even if there
is no word in human language or thought in the
human heart which answers even by analogy to
the Divine as it really is, still there exists in man
a necessary relation or " *habitudo* " towards
which he must act, in reference to which he must
think, either consistently and on a plan or without
any plan and in despair. He *has* acted towards it

It is, above all, that the Eastern religions do not make their essential note Catholicity, the including the whole nature of man. At this point we may add that the argument mentioned by Sir L. Stephen may be turned round and looked at the other way. Easterns themselves allow that the points in which Christendom is superior are points which man owes to Christianity; while Catholics are ready to allow that the points in which the West is inferior to the East are points in which the eastern character of Christianity has not yet been sufficiently realized.

The Church, then, standing between God and man, represents both the negative and affirmative results of man's thought and finds both alike necessary to the great religious process in humanity. As representing man before God, she says: " In that I have sought Thee I have already found Thee." As representing God to man— whether the individual or the race, whether the result of his thought has been affirmative or negative she says: " In that thou hast sought Him, thou hast already found Him."

NEWMAN, PASCAL, LOISY AND THE CATHOLIC CHURCH.

PART II

(1).—THE ACTUAL POSITION OF THE CHURCH.

Is there, then, no such thing as a corruption in the Catholic Church? Must every development be a true one and must the accepted, the popular, the conventional view of religion always be the true one and the personal view the false?

No man has suffered more than Newman from this misapprehension of his argument in the Essay on Development. " A popular religion," he says, " will always be corrupt," and the Catholic religion is popular and will, therefore, as a popular religion, be corrupt.

The fact of applying tests to religion—the fact of applying tests to the development of the Catholic Church is, in itself, an appeal to the reason and conscience of individuals; and the Church has never disdained the use of argument or denied that her authority can only be defended by reason.

The Church does not exist to destroy, but to call forth, to exercise and to educate reason. But she demands that she should herself be regarded, at least, as a natural product; as a social phenomenon, in accordance with the needs, capacities, and social habitudes of man; and no man has a right to begin by assuming that she is outside the usual tests of

truth because she claims a supernatural origin or
that her unity is no argument for her internal consistency because it is but the result of coercion.
She does not deny that she is a subject for historical
criticism, or rational enquiry; but she demands
that, as in a natural phenomenon, the fact that she
answers to some necessity of nature and has a
meaning in the system of things shall be clearly
apprehended by her critics or their criticism will be
pointless and futile. Her doctrines and her
development must be regarded as, in the first place,
a natural process and not criticized from the first as
an artificial growth, the invention of priests and a
means of blinding the people.

After such inquiry has been made and such
criticism has been attempted, it may be discovered
that an artificial and coercive despotism, founded
upon the inventions of priests, has been the true
cause of the Church's enduring life and wide
popularity. But this not very probable conclusion
is too often regarded as a premiss, and a philosopher like Mr. Morley does not hesitate to speak of
the doctrine of future reward and punishment—one
of the most ancient in the world—as if it had been
the arbitrary invention of priests and had no roots
and no growth from the very base and heart of
human nature. In the name of truth such philosophers denounce Christian dogma as a legend; but
in so doing they give an importance and validity to
falsehood which can be convincing to none but
sentimentalists.

The Church, then, does not regard herself as

perfect, but as having found the only possible way in which to make a great religious experiment, to organize and objectify the religious idea; to create and to continue an organism in which the religious process may be carried on. She does not say that she has accomplished her purpose in a manner the most perfect that could be conceived—far from it, she does but say, that she has done what she could; but she adds that if she has failed in her purpose it is not easy to see whom else she should regard as having succeeded, nor is it easy to find in the world an organism which has united experiment, consistency and advance in the religious idea, in an equal degree with herself.

She does not profess to have attained perfection or to have come to the end of her development, or to have lived out in its fulness, or as yet to be able to express " the main idea " of Christ. She has implicitly allowed—nay earnestly insisted on, the moral and intellectual imperfection from which she has suffered, in the fact that she commissioned the schoolmen to set forth in a new form the whole of her teaching and encouraged the Saints to reform, exhort, rebuke and train her people. She does not exist to coerce the intellect and will of the individual or to repress the conclusions of reason or to force mankind into an arbitrary unity. If coercion she has employed; if repression she has exercised; and thereby weakened the argument derived from an intrinsic and voluntary unity it was, at any rate, on behalf of that very progress which she seemed to prevent and in condemnation of that very finality

which she seemed to profess that time has shown
her to have acted For, as a fact, she has been in
religion, the natural ground for *that struggle for
existence between ideas,* that struggle between the
past and the present, and that struggle between
authority and the individual in which alone a survival of the fittest becomes possible, and order and
continuity are united with progress, advance and
development.

Outside the Church the struggle of ideas on the
subject of religions has either become an endless ·
controversy, as in the Protestant Churches, or has
practically ceased, as in the Greek Church; while
the purely intellectual discussion of religion has
but given birth to theories which ever more tend to
justify the course of purely religious development
in the Church.

In this manner, every kind of idea—
(Platonism, the Aristotelianism of the schools, the
license of the Renaissance, the Puritanism of the
Reaction, liberty and necessity, and an endless host
of speculative philosophies) has been given a part
in a struggle which is still going on ; because only
those which can prove their consistency with the
continued vitality of the organism can ultimately
survive, unless they succeed in killing the organism
itself.

Now an organism must die that it may live ;—
must change that it may endure. The question is,
have the changes in the Church been corruptions or
have they been changes which are necessary to
growth ?

No one denies that some kind of vitality exists in the Church and no one denies that there is some kind of corruption.   Is this a religious vitality and is it a vitality which shows itself consistent *in type* with that religious life whence it professes to be derived and on which it professes to be founded—the Christian religion as set forth by Christ?   In the attempt to sum up and reconcile all religions and the whole religious idea has not the profounder religion been lost sight of and some sort of Paganism survived? or has not the Christian type, at least, been modified to the advantage of a type opposed to it?

So great an authority as Harnack adds his testimony to that of the Protestant communions by declaring that it has; that the Christian religion in the Catholic Church has become a cult, and that this is the very sort of religion which Christ came to destroy.

It has been said that every kind of religion must have the defect of its qualities.   The vice of a subjective religion will be fanaticism; the vice of a religion which makes self-renunciation its chief object and insists on tradition will be superstition. From these defects will arise the kind of popular corruption incidental to the greatest religions from the very fact that they are popular.

Matthew Arnold considered that Proestantism had got the method of Jesus—His earnestness and inwardness; that Catholicism had kept His secret of self-renunciation and gentleness; and that both had lost, except in the greatest of the saints, His reasonableness.

This representation of the matter is probably not far from the truth and it is borne out by Kant, who says that the defect of Protestantism has been fanaticism and the defect of Catholicism superstition, and this, from the nature of the case because the defect of an individualistic religion could hardly fail to be fanaticism and the defect of a social religion superstition.

But, if these are defects, they are, without doubt, the defects of qualities; and where the defects do not exist we shall hardly be likely to find the qualities, that is the religious spirit itself.

It is not, therefore, a very profound objection to a popular religion that it is a cult and has become superstitious, because a popular religion which has any life at all must be a cult, and will be sure to have those corruptions which arise from its characteristic defect, for a popular religion, says Newman, will always be corrupt.

The real objection would be founded on the completeness of this corruption and on the depth of this superstition. It must needs be that corruption should follow both the extension and the intensification of religion : the question is whether there was at the same time a development.

If Harnack is objecting to a religion becoming a cult and to a cult simply as such, the objection (as the Abbé Loisy observes) is really an objection to the social nature of man. If he is only objecting to the kind of superstition which is sure to exist in a popular religion, he is objecting to a religion be-coming popular.   But if he means that the Catholic Church by her teaching has encouraged supersti-tion for its own sake and has so enlarged its sway that true Christianity is in danger of perishing altogether, the point becomes a question of fact and we must inquire what sort of example the Church holds up to imitation and what kind of teaching she imparts.

Now, it is surely a significant fact that it should be in a Church which is considered to have so far forsaken the special teaching of the Gospel, *rather than among those who made it their boast to have returned to the Gospel* that those Saints who are considered by modern writers of all schools best to represent the spirit of Christ have, somehow or another, continued to arise.   " There is more of Jesus," says Matthew Arnold, " in the little finger of St. Theresa, than in the whole body of John Knox."   Nor can so Evangelical a writer as Sir James Stephen find any character in the Protestant world which so kindles his religious enthusiasm as the character of St. Francis Xavier.   It is a Protes-tant writer in France who speaks in the same terms of St. Francis of Assisi.   It is Carducci in Italy who adds his testimony to that of Sabatier.   It is Castellar in Spain who adds his testimony to that of Carducci.   It is the Positivist Cotter Morrison who gives a like position to St. Bernard.

If the Church, then, has among her people fallen so far into superstition as to fall away from Christ, it is not for want of a remedy within Herself nor for want of the spirit of Christ in her teaching. Not only have these Saints been in great part at least the direct result of her teaching—but their lives are themselves a part of Her teaching and their writings are commended to the perusal, and their sanctity to the imitation, of all Catholic peoples. It is in vain to say that the Saints are the exception which prove the rule and that the Church is but building the sepulchres of her prophets in commending them, for she does not cease preaching in their very words and insisting daily on their example.

It would seem, then, that the superstition which exists and whose existence no one denies, how little so ever we may wish to defend it, or to excuse it, is but a part of that corruption inevitable to a popular religion and does not arise from, and is not of so gross a kind as to be characteristic of, an inward apostacy from the teaching and example of Jesus; but that, on the contrary, in spite of Her acknowledged developments and Her assimilation of that which is without, She still produces something which at any rate appears to persons who are not Catholics at all, more like the teaching and secret of Jesus than is to be found in reformed and Evangelical communions.

The Catholic religion, then, cannot rightly be said to have become a mere cult; to have fallen so far into superstition as to have lost the Christian type; to have so modified Christian teaching in the attempt (whether conscious or not) to reconcile all religions to itself, as to have become but a Chris-

tianised Paganism; to have become, in short, the
very sort of religion which Christ came to destroy.

But it is a question whether there is any kind of
religion which Christ came on earth to destroy.
He said Himself that He had come not to destroy
but to fulfil, nor did He treat the most superstitious expression of the religious spirit in the
woman who hoped to be healed by the very touch of
His garment as a matter for rebuke or contempt.

And the Church in dealing with Pagan nations
—when she adopted much of their language, many
of their rites and something of their ethos—was
but following the example of her Master and refusing to convert by the imposition of ideas solely as
from above. By thus acting perhaps she gained
something for herself as well as for the converts
who approached her. She acted on the principle
that the Christian religion contained the deepest
truth and ultimate unity of religious thought, but
that other religions also contained something that
was true. " Dig deep enough," said the greatest
of her Doctors, " into the human and you will find
the Divine."

The freedom to use Pagan ceremonies and to
adopt something that remained of Pagan philosophy may have had its dangers and its scandals; but
it was a freedom that had been slowly acquired by
the ever increasing consciousness of the sove-
reignty, centrality and depth of the Christian
religion. It was only by experience that the deeper
meaning of Pagan thought and custom could be
fully understood; and then it sometimes appeared

as if it was rather the fear of idols than the use of images which was a sign of an idolatrous habit of mind. When the Christian religion, by gathering into its embrace those who had had inner experience of Pagan worship, had ceased to be a party or a school or a sect, and had become a " world religion " it could regard all religions as in some degree expressions of its spirit and elaborations of its thought.

As I said just now that you cannot have the qualities of religion unless you have the defects—so now I add unless you have the corruptions you cannot have the developments: for it is of the very Pagan stuff out of which the corruption was made that the development became possible.

By a slow process; by the influence of one man here and another there; by the conversion of a philosopher in one place; by the gradual influx of the simpler Pagan crowd in another, the Christian Church came to inherit some of the deeper spiritual riches of the Gentiles; and, though sometimes at the cost of the individual here and there, the society gained the liberty, by giving Paganism a deeper interpretation, to use it in the service of Christ. The religious idea was compelled for many a year to travel along a narrow way, but it was brought forth at last into a wealthy place.

Therefore, that Catholicity, which at first did but mean the collection of traditions from all parts within the Christian Church, came to mean what it was inevitable in the nature of the case it should, from the first, actually imply,—the bringing into one and gathering together of all the strongest facts and experiences of religion,—all elements in the religious idea wherever found which could prove their fitness by survival or their vitality by their growth or this " richness " by their capacity for a deeper interpretation;—all " truths of religion," outside the Christian Church as well as within it. In this manner and on a basis of the deeper expediency, begun but not completed, attempted not achieved, a Catholic Church has alone any chance of becoming " Humanity grown conscious of itself."

It is often the poor and the simple, with a few isolated scholars and mystics, who are the first to realize and to feel the benefits of this triumphant freedom. Untroubled by intellectualism or pietism, untrammelled by controversy and the mere appearance of consistency they have found pleasure in all that gives aid to their religious aspiration; and as to the pure all things are pure, so for them, without a thought of exterior consistency, an inner and deeper consistency of the spirit has been formed.

And it has been from this cause, rather than from her theological development that we are able to regard the church as " the fullest exponent and transmitter of life " in the world; not as she appears in controversy laden with texts and shackled with scholastic logic, though even there she sometimes takes a wider sweep and makes for a higher goal; not as she appears in Councils, in Synods, and in Congregations, though there also she has a vivid inspiration;

N

but in the full stream of her magnificent progress and with her people's shout of triumph in her ears; for there it is she is seen to be greater than the Ideals of the older civilisation, not because she has destroyed them, but because, set on the highest throne that she can offer, they are no longer rivals of the majesty of Christ.

It is because the throne of Christ is conceived as founded in the deepest part of man's nature, that it can thus be raised above all principalities and powers; and it is in the Church's recognition of the intrinsic glory of Christianity that her own glory altogether lies. She could never have shewn her confidence in the incommunicable greatness of Christ had she continued for ever blind to the intrinsic greatness of Pagan ideals or regarded the gods of the heathen as, in her first impulse and onset, she had been compelled to regard them. Christ's triumph must be shown to be no mere military victory in which opponents are not only vanquished but annihilated. The victory must be one in which all rivalry ceases because all that is great in the enemy is both transcended and absorbed.

Not yet can that victory be won; not yet has every enemy been thus brought into the embrace of God. But if " morality is " indeed " the nature of things "; if " the greatest thoughts come from the heart "; if it is from living out the true life that religious truth may best be secured; and if the saints are those who have had a genius for morality, that Church may, surely, be said to have got nearest the nature of things, nearest the objective ground and basis of religion, which, with so full a recognition of Pagan worship and Pagan thought as to cause scandal to her enemies, has been able to produce the saints whom men, of whatever creed, have felt to be the highest and the best representatives of the spirit of Christ.

If that victory is ever to be won, here alone is the promise and the presage of our winning it. If the throne of Christ is founded not only in the hearts of a Judaized Christendom but in the heart of human nature itself, then it is not by a constant return to Primitive Ages or by a deeper interpretation of Hebrew prophets—how necessary soever in its place that return and that interpretation may be, —but by bringing the living Christian spirit, in its spontaneous growth, into contact with the living spirit of man and finding how, of its own nature and from its intrinsic depth, it goes beneath, absorbs and outdoes all the aspirations of the old religions—summing them up, explaining, transcending and uniting them—that the first steps in religious development must be made.

If it is a religion, which fills to the utmost edge and touches at its centre, the heart of humanity, that is necessary for man; if it is in the fact that the heart of man is naturally Christian that the deepest argument for Christianity lies; if it is in order that man, whether Jew or Greek, whether Protestant or Catholic, whether of the ancient or the modern spirit, should be enabled to realize his complete ideals, find the basis of his deepest

thought and transend them both, that God is conceived as becoming man; if it is not by an isolated
and circumscribed following of Christ—in the
course of His life during the few years of His
struggle with the Jews—that this universal spirit is
to be attained and that man can be conceived as becoming God; but by taking the whole life of man
and finding its interpretation and its basis in the
universal and ever deepening consciousness of the
Christian ideal; if Christ is indeed the God of
humanity, then what He said of the religion of the
Jews, He must be conceived as saying of all
national and all ancient religions:—That He was
not come to destroy but to complete; that not one
jot of those laws, those hopes and those ideals
should fail but that every one of them should be
fulfilled.

(2).—THE IDEAL OF THE CHURCH.

THE TRUTH WHICH MAKES MAN FREE.

If it is true that " *morality is the nature of things* " and that the saints are persons who have " *a genius for morality*," it is clear that the best way to get at the nature of things is through the morality of the saints. Again, if it is through the Church that humanity is to become completely conscious of itself ; and if it is only through the nature of things that this end can be attained, the Church has not done amiss in giving so high a place to sanctity. But religion, which is the immediate concern of the saints, has been called " morality, touched with emotion " ; while, according to Newman, it is anterior to morality, what brought morality into being, and the natural reformer, not only of men's morals, but of their very conceptions of morality. Thus it would be to the saints that man should have recourse if he wishes to find experimentally the true place of religion in the order of his being. The Church, then, in the attempt to accomplish the great purpose of making humanity conscious of itself, was compelled to become, in the first place, the exponent and interpreter of religion and the organism in which the religious process should be carried on, and could scarcely do otherwise than entrust her reform, her preservation and the methods of her action to the saints rather than to persons of any other kind of excellence. Nor have some of the most determined among her opponents denied that the persons, to whom she has given so high a place and made the leaders in the great work which she has endeavoured to achieve, were, for the most part, worthy of the honour.

But, in order that humanity may attain complete consciousness of itself, nothing is more certain than that the intellect must have freedom and the power to use, in all directions, the whole of its resources. No one will deny that where the intellect is dead, there can be no other kind of life. It was from the fact that religion and morality were given by experience the very office of keeping the balance of man's nature and holding him true to it, that the Church came to possess any authority at all. If it should turn out, then, that the rule of sanctity has resulted in the collapse of intellect, the value of sanctity, in bringing about the great object of the Church, would be open to serious question. If sanctity is indeed a genius for the nature of things, and if the Church has ruled in accordance with the genius of the saints, intellect ought to be more completely liberated in the Church than outside it. Now, in her ideal, the Church has set up sanctity as her first object, and acted on the assumption that if men seek first the Kingdom of God and His righteousness, all other things shall be added to them. To those who do the will is made the promise that they shall know the doctrine

and philosophers who have studied the lives of
the saints and the nature of sanctity, from their
very desire to deny to sanctity a supernatural
origin, ..ave found themselves compelled to admit
that the saints, nevertheless, hold a position which
is but their due, because morality is the nature
of things and sanctity is a genius for morality.
Such philosophers have perceived, too, that as the
variety in the character of sanctity gives the colour
to life, and as each saint contributes a colour of his
own, the union of all these in one Church which attempts to amalgamate them, may give that one
light clear and dry which is the truth in the region
of morals and religion.   That division between the
higher nature and the lower, the spiritual and the
material, to which these philosophers justly object
in speculation, they are ready to allow, has been
experimentally established and rightly acted on by
the saints, for even if there has been exaggeration
in the sacrifice of the lower and the material, they
maintain that without taking this kind of risk, the
greatest triumphs humanity has won could never
have been possible.   So far all is simple and clear
enough.   But, when the saints are taken as themselves witnesses to the truth of the Catholic religion
these philosophers reply that the Church has never
properly made the truth an end; the truth has been
regarded as a means and sanctity itself as the end.
As there is a considerable difference of opinion
among men in regard to what truth is, these philosophers do not, for the most part, attempt to show
that there is a truth which the Church has

notoriously failed to attain, but they assert that
official theologians have ever stood in the way of
scientific progress and that the intellectual vitality
of Catholics is a low one.   This fact, they think, is
enough to show that truth and the intellect have
been neglected and even opposed by the Church.
They acknowledge that the Church has produced
in sanctity the finest flower of religious humanity,
and that, in so doing, she has made a vast contribution to religious truth.   They do not even go so
far as to argue that the saints belong to the world
and, therefore, are in no special sense witnesses to
the truth of Catholicism.   They allow that it is the
very fact that the saints have significance for all
the world which makes their significance, as witnesses to Catholicism, so far as it goes, valid for
all the world.   But they complain that the Church,
having had the best opportunity for gathering the
religious advantages which sanctity offers, has
failed to reap those advantages and has left the task
to philosophy and science.   And the reason why
the Church has failed, they consider to be the fact
that she has discouraged all originality of thought,
condemned all the movements which have arisen
within her towards a modern systematization of her
principles, and acted, in the sphere of intellect, in
a manner directly opposed to the very axioms of
life which she might have learnt, and which she
has actually taught, from the lives of the saints.
The saints refused to break the bruised reed or
quench the smoking flax, and, with regard to the
moral life, the Church which taught the saints,

has generally acted as they acted; but in the life
of the intellect, it is said, she has acted on an
opposite principle and invariably broken, when she
could, the bruised reed and quenched the smoking
flax.

In the moral and religious life, the saints have
often been allowed a freedom which even Macaulay
can praise as the result of politic prudence and a
far-seeing wisdom; but in the life of the intellect we
look in vain for " the liberty wherewith Christ " is
said to have " made man free."   In the breadth,
variety, boldness and independence of the action
of the saints, we find a testimony to the freedom of
the City of God, and in this freedom we cannot but
recognise a note of the Church of humanity; but,
in the region of the intellect, the Church has
imitated the rule of the Cæsars rather than the rule
of the saints and lorded it over the flock of Christ.

Now we cannot, consistently with Christian
teaching, deny that in order to realise to the full
the ideal of Christ, the whole man must be free
and that, in order to realise the ideal of the Church,
the Church on earth, like that Jerusalem which is
above, must be free, and that, in this sense, freedom
is a note of the true Church. Christ did not come
only to liberate man from the false Sabbath of the
Rabbis, but from all the false Sabbaths which have
interdicted the healthful and beneficent energies of
man, whether in his practical or in his intellectual
life. Were the Church to be represented only by
the Inquisition, the Congregations and the Index,

or even as a purely clerical institution, her cause
could be defended, at this day, by few. But here,
it must be allowed to be a significant fact that, in
spite of the narrowness of theologians, it has been
in the Catholic Church, and not in communions
which are supposed to have given most freedom
to the intellect, that the pioneers in modern
philosophy and modern criticism, Descartes and
Simon, did actually arise. If the intellectual
vitality of the Catholic Church had to be tested by
the breadth of thought and depth of insight shown
by official theologians, it would seem like irony to
cite these great names in her defence. But official
theologians are, from the necessity of the case, only
one element, and that the conservative element, in
the Church. Their duty is to preserve the consistency of the Church's teaching. To expect among
officials like these, instances of progress or proofs
of advance, would be like expecting an intelligence
such as that of Lord Eldon, the greatest of English
constitutional lawyers, to provide an instance of
the progressive spirit of the English constitution.
It may be admitted that official authority in the
Church has exceeded the privilege of officials to
be obstructive; that officials have done all that in
them lay to represent the unity of the Church, not
as a spontaneous unity arising from the depth and
vitality of her teaching, but as an artificial
uniformity brought about by tyranny and coercion.
It may be admitted that, by their condemnation
of so vast a number of philosophers, theologians
and critics, they have at the present day brought

about a deadlock between thought and religion, and reduced authority to impotence. It were indeed vain to deny that there are officials who act as if they thought that the strength of an executive consisted in pushing its claims with peremptory violence and straining prerogative till it snaps. But these facts, which few deny, do but afford a clearer evidence how stupendous must be the vitality, and how profound the inward unity, of the Church, when even such a strain as this has not been able to suppress the one or to dissolve the other. If, in spite of this intolerant narrowness and this direct discouragement of all originality of thought; if, in spite of so rigid a conservatism and the avowed attempt to attain, by coercion, a merely external uniformity, some of the most original minds in the world have nevertheless appeared in the Church and thought it worth while rather to suffer persecution within than seek an individualistic liberty outside, it is surely a proof of the depth and vitality of an inward unity which none but the ignorant could confound with the uniformity of the drill-sergeant and the schoolmaster. A peremptory spirit in authority has done all that could be done by interdict, by threat and by terror to turn the unity of the Church into some such rigid uniformity as this; but the more resolutely the attempt has been made, only the more clearly has it been proved by the result that a deeper unity exists in spite of the officials—a unity which defies them now and will be their condemnation hereafter.

A witness to this intrinsic and free unity of thought in the Church do these great liberating spirits inevitably form. The point on which I am insisting is, not only that Descartes could find in the Catholic Church and nowhere else the basis for his " morale pour provision," or that Simon could find in its living authority the only security that a free criticism would not dissolve the Christian society ; but that it is in the Catholic Church rather than in any other community that these first liberators of human thought should have actually arisen. Nor is it only by Descartes and Simon that this point is illustrated. The breath of the Time-spirit, which has destroyed the religious significance of so vast a number of Protestant writers about religion, has not only preserved but added to the significance of Catholic writers on religion, to that of Bossuet in his broad and massive treatment of society ; to that of Pascal in his treatment of Christian apologetic ; to that of More, Erasmus, Tauler, Mabillon, Maldonatus, and Fénelon.

It would not be too much to say that the kind of intellectual unity which subsists between these writers, so essentially different in temperament, is the firmest basis for hope in the intellectual progress of man in matters of religion which it is possible to find in the history of Christendom.

Can it be said that those Anglican and Protestant divines upon whom Mark Pattison and Matthew Arnold alike consider that the breath of the Time-spirit has blown, perished because they deserved to perish, or that they failed from some intrinsic defect of intellect or of learning? Can it be said that Bull, Waterland, Thorndyke, Barrow, Tillotson, Sherlock, Stillingfleet were wanting in learning or in ability sufficient to cope with the problems before them? No, it cannot be said even of Tillotson, nor in the long run is it possible to doubt that some of them will receive in a larger Catholicism what is but their due, a recognised place in the City of God for which they laboured.

But, that men may acquire universal recognition and permanence, there must be some definite line of orientation on which they work; and, great as the contribution of these men sometimes was to polemic and to learning, they were so far hampered by their position as to fail to rise to the height which the argument required or to deal with great subjects greatly. They could defend a special rendering of Christianity with masculine vigour and acuteness, but they dared not make use of any positive development or take any positive line of advance. They had destroyed too much already to make progress on their own account, and progress along a definite line is necessary if any permanent advantage is to be gained.

But there cannot be any progress without some kind of continuity; there cannot be advance without some kind of consistency; there cannot be developement without some means of relating the present to the past. In the sciences, continuity is preserved by the consensus of opinion and by the testimony of the facts; but, in religion, the facts are only known through the testimony of ages to the exigencies of man's nature and through the test of experiment made upon the use of the testimony; and the facts, concerned as they are with so delicate and subtle a subject as the religious nature of man, can only be treated as facts, when, through consistency and coherence, they have arrived at some objective expression.

If, then, Catholic writers on religion have been able to avoid the provincialism into which other religious writers have fallen; if Catholic writers have displayed a certain universatility of spirit, which makes them significant for all time, and Protestant writers have been too negative, too controversial and even too conservative, is it not because the Church secures a consistent basis, a basis of spiritual fact, a mode of continuity, a mode of relating the present with the past, which makes a bolder progress possible and, in the long run, a truer liberation of the mind? Is it not because a consistent objective basis, however crude or vague, is essential to progress itself and so to any intellectual freedom of real value or universal validity? Had this consistency of basis been of a nature intrinsically false or opposed to the nature of things, it would have destroyed this significance and imperilled this duration. But the fact that these writers show signs of an indefinite endurance and ever increasing significance is surely a proof that the basis on which they build is in accordance with the nature of things.

Writers of the 18th century did the world an invaluable service by showing how little religious truth is truth in historical detail or veracity in physical fact.   But the 18th century writers dismissed as so much rubbish, not only the physical phenomena of the mystics but that kind of truth of which these phenomena were but the vehicle or symbol.   Now, then, that men have come to see that the kind of truth which lay beneath is concerned with their happiness, with their " living from the greatest depths of being ' and that " sanctity is a genius for morality," the fact that Catholic writers on religion have still a significance for religious minds of every communion is beginning to be accounted for.   The Catholic writers whom ⊥ have mentioned were as little concerned with mystical phenomena as the writers of the 18th century.   But the kind of truth that lay beneath—this they trusted, this they expounded, this they enforced.

But, it is a still further testimony to the truth of this underlying consistency, that, in accordance with it, some of these wrters were able to make an actual advance in the intellectual appreciation of religion.   The greater Protestant and Positivist philosophers, who have dealt with the subject, have united in showing that these Catholic writers were not Protestant reformers born out of due time or sceptical philosophers in disguise, but as profoundly Catholic in religion as they were free in criticism and that they, one and all, considered the Catholic Church the only kind of authority consistent with the full use of such freedom. To these writers the testimony of authority to the religious exigencies of man was not a fetter to bind them but a light to inform them; not an obstacle to progress but a basis on which alone progress became possible; not a means of narrowing the spirit but the very cause of their freedom from the narrowness of sect.

In Erasmus and Malonatus and Simon, in Astruc, Geddes and the Bollandists, a steady advance has been made in criticism both of Church and Bible, without breaking up the kind of authority in religion or lessening that seriousness in its teaching, upon which the majority of mankind must depend; nay, such writers as Mabillon and Pascal and Fenelon have added to the weight of authority at the very time that they have diminished its crudities.

In these writers a clear and definite line of orientation has been taken; and, through their means, a progress has been made in religion which is no mere indefinite movement, and an authority has been set up which is no mere tyranny, but one which, as the grounds of scientific criticism become objectively clear, can put away for ever the crudities which belong to the childhood of the race.

By one of those paradoxical coincidences, which abound in history, it so happens that Bossuet who condemned the Biblical criticism of Pere Simon, was the first historian to make a philosophic